Samuel Macpherson Janney

Peace Principles Exemplified in the Early History of Pennsylvania

Samuel Macpherson Janney

Peace Principles Exemplified in the Early History of Pennsylvania

ISBN/EAN: 9783337222413

Printed in Europe, USA, Canada, Australia, Japan

Cover: Foto ©ninafisch / pixelio.de

More available books at **www.hansebooks.com**

PEACE PRINCIPLES

EXEMPLIFIED

IN THE

EARLY HISTORY OF PENNSYLVANIA.

BY

SAMUEL M. JANNEY,

AUTHOR OF THE "LIFE OF WILLIAM PENN," "LIFE OF GEORGE FOX,"
"HISTORY OF FRIENDS," ETC., ETC.

Blessed are the peacemakers, for they shall be called the children
of God.—MATT. v. 9.
The work of righteousness shall be peace; and the effect of righteousness,
quietness and assurance forever.—ISAIAH xxxii. 17.

PHILADELPHIA:
FRIENDS' BOOK ASSOCIATION,
706 ARCH STREET.
1876.

Entered according to Act of Congress in the year 1876, by the
FRIENDS' BOOK ASSOCIATION OF PHILADELPHIA,
in the Office of the Librarian of Congress, at Washington, D.C.

PREFACE.

IN this centennial year, when the representatives of nearly all civilized nations will meet in the city of Brotherly Love, and engage in harmonious intercourse, it seems to be an appropriate season to revive the memory of the Founder of Pennsylvania, and to illustrate the principles of peace.

There is, in thoughtful minds throughout Christendom, a growing disposition to consider the best means of averting the dreadful calamities of war, and the oppression that results from maintaining vast armaments in time of peace. But we must not expect the rulers of nations to reform these evils until the people shall demand it, nor will the people demand it until they are more generally enlightened and imbued with Christian principles.

A good work is being done by the Peace Societies in this country, and in Europe. Their publications have thrown a flood of light upon the enormous evils of war, and the means that may be used to secure the blessings of peace. They have shown that International arbitration has, in many instances, succeeded in settling disputes that endangered the peace of nations, and that a code of International laws, administered by a High Court of Nations, would be the means of preserving peaceful relations, and leading to a general disarmament throughout Christendom.

They have called in earnest language upon the ministers and members of Christian Churches to proclaim and to practise the *Law of Love* as taught and exemplified by the Author of our religion, a law that is no less imperative upon nations than upon individuals, which would lead to the reign of universal peace as foretold by the prophet, when "nation shall not lift up sword against nation, neither shall they learn war any more."

My design, in this work, is to give a concise account of the only attempt that has ever been made to govern a commonwealth on the principles enunciated by our Saviour, in His Sermon on the Mount, and to show that the reign of "peace on earth, and good will to men," is not only beautiful in theory, but feasible in practice.

It will be observed that a portion of the materials used in this essay are reproduced from my work entitled "The Life of William Penn, with Selections from his Correspondence and Autobiography," to which the reader is referred for further particulars relating to the early history of Pennsylvania.

SAMUEL M. JANNEY.

LINCOLN, LOUDOUN COUNTY, VIRGINIA.
THIRD MONTH, FIRST, 1876.

TABLE OF CONTENTS.

INTRODUCTION.

FIRST EUROPEAN SETTLEMENTS ON THE DELAWARE.

1623-1677.

Dutch settlement—Fort Nassau—Captain Mey—De Vrie's colony at Hoor-kills—Destroyed by Indians—Swedish colony and fort at Christina—At Tinicum—Colonel John Printz—Warlike measures—The Dutch build Fort Cassimer—The Swedes subdued—Dutch policy—The English take possession for the Duke of York—Disastrous results of military sway 11

CHAPTER I.

BIRTH AND EDUCATION OF WILLIAM PENN—SETTLEMENT OF NEW JERSEY.

1644-1678.

Penn at Oxford—Religious impressions—Tour of Europe—Sent to Ireland—Military expedition—Preaching of Thomas Loe—Penn convinced of Friends' principles—Displeasure of his father—Penn becomes an author—Imprisoned in the Tower—Released—Arrested at a Friends' meeting—Trial of Penn and Mead—Their imprisonment—Penn pleads for liberty of conscience—Death of his father—Colonization of New Jersey 25

CHAPTER II.

COLONIZATION OF PENNSYLVANIA.

1680-1682.

William Penn petitions Charles II. for territory on the Delaware—The royal patent for Pennsylvania—Penn's letter to the inhabitants—His care for the Indians—His letter to them—Arrival of colonists—Penn's views on government—The first constitution—Grant of territory by Duke of York—Penn's instructions to his children—His arrival at New Castle—He reaches Philadelphia—Meets the Indians—Plan of the city—Visits New York—Account of the great treaty at Shackamaxon.. 37

CHAPTER III.

LEGISLATION—AND INTERCOURSE WITH INDIANS.

1682-1683.

First assembly—Code of laws—Assembly in Philadelphia—New Charter—Purchase of Indian lands—The long walk—Trial for witchcraft and acquittal—Rapid increase of population—Character of colonists—Indian traits... 65

CHAPTER IV.

THE BOUNDARY QUESTION—REVOLUTION IN ENGLAND

1684-1689.

Controversy with Lord Baltimore about boundaries—Penn's return to England—The boundary question considered—Death of Charles II.—Accession of James II.—Release of Friends from prison—Affairs of Pennsylvania—Unpopularity of the king—His abdication—William and Mary crowned—William Penn arrested—Cleared in open court—Act of toleration—Blackwell appointed governor—His resignation—Indian alarm 83

CHAPTER V.

TROUBLES IN EUROPE AND AMERICA.

1689-1695.

War in Europe—Penn arrested and discharged—Funeral of George Fox—Penn lives in seclusion—Affairs of Pennsylvania—Separation of territories—George Keith's separation—William Penn deprived of his government—He is cleared by the king—Penn's maxims—His essay towards the present and future peace of Europe...................... 98

CHAPTER VI.

COLONIAL AFFAIRS—PENN'S REMOVAL TO THE COLONY.

1693-1701.

Governor Fletcher's administration—Military services demanded—Perplexity of the assembly—Restoration of the government to Penn—Markham deputy-governor—Prosperity of the colony—Penn's second marriage—Death of his son—Travels as a minister—Embarks for Pennsylvania—Arrival—James Logan secretary—Penn's concern for the blacks and Indians—Rise of testimony against slavery—Its progress—Penn liberates his slaves—Pennsbury manor—Indian councils—The king's requisition for money to build forts—Motion in Parliament to annex proprietary governments to the crown—Indian visitors—Assembly meets—New constitution—Friends' public school—Penn and family return to England 114

CHAPTER VII.

PENN'S PECUNIARY EMBARRASSMENTS.

1702-1709.

Death of King William and accession of Queen Anne—Penn in favor at court—Affairs of Pennsylvania—Governor Hamilton—The church party—Colonel Quarry—Penn's pecuniary wants—He proposes to sell his government to the crown—Governor Evans and William Penn, Jr., in Pennsylvania—Evans' proclamation for a militia—False alarm and illegal exactions of Governor Evans—Removal of Evans and appointment of Governor Gookin—Penn's imprisonment for debt—His release. 135

CHAPTER VIII.
THE LAST DAYS OF PENN.
1709–1718.

Dissensions between the council and assembly—Requisitions for military purposes—Rejected by the assembly—Contest between David Lloyd and James Logan—Logan goes to England and is acquitted—Reaction in Pennsylvania in favor of the Proprietary—Harmony restored—Subsidy granted to the queen—Act to prevent the importation of negroes—Penn's proposed sale of his government—He is stricken with paralysis—His death and character.............................. 152

CHAPTER IX.
THE PEACE-POLICY A SUCCESS.

Difficulties encountered by Penn—Wars of the other colonies—Feasibility of peace-principles—Political contests in all free governments—Feudalism and democracy incompatible—Death penalty not inflicted—Intercourse with Indians—Testimony of C. Sumner in favor of peace. 162

INTRODUCTION.

FIRST EUROPEAN SETTLEMENTS ON THE DELAWARE.

1623-1677.

THE colonization and early history of Pennsylvania, under the government of its illustrious founder, is a subject of deep interest to reflecting minds, affording instructive evidence of the blessings derived from religious liberty and the practical observance of Christian principles.

The entire absence of military defences, the enjoyment of uninterrupted peace, the freedom and liberality of her institutions, the patriarchal simplicity of manners united with moral refinement, and the unexampled rapidity of her growth, are features that cannot be found so happily blended in the history of any other people.

It is the purpose of this work to furnish a condensed statement of the government established and the principles maintained by the colonists who were engaged with William Penn in his noble enterprise, and as a preliminary to this design a brief notice of the earlier European settlements on the banks of the Delaware is deemed appropriate.

The first of those settlements was planted by the Dutch in the year 1623, under the command of Captain Cornelius Jacobson Mey, who sailed up the Delaware to the vicinity of Gloucester Point, and "on the eastern shore commenced the erection of Fort Nassau, as well for security against the Indians as for a trading-post with them." *

The measures pursued by the Dutch in erecting forts and exhibiting the implements of war, were in striking contrast with the peaceable policy afterwards pursued by Penn and his associates, and the results that ensued furnish a cogent argument in favor of peace principles.

The expedition under the command of Captain Mey was sent out by the Dutch West India Company with a view to establishing a fur trade with the natives. It appears that the enterprise was not successful; most of the colonists abandoned the fort, and after a lapse of ten years it was found in possession of the Indians.

In 1630, the Dutch West India Company sent out two vessels under the command of De Vries,

---

* Hazard's "Annals of Pennsylvania," p. 13.

who, in the following year, founded a colony near Cape Henlopen, on Lewis's Creek, which he named Hoorn-kill, probably from the place of his residence, Hoorn, a port in Holland. Here he built a trading-house or fort, defended by a palisade. After a short stay he returned to Holland, leaving the colony, consisting of more than thirty persons, under the command of Giles Osset.

During the absence of De Vries his lieutenant quarrelled with the Indians. One of their chiefs was killed in the affray, and the friends of the murdered chief attacked the fort and put all the colonists to death.

On the return of De Vries with others the following year a melancholy spectacle was presented to their view. "They found their dwelling-house and store had been burnt to the ground and their fortification utterly destroyed. But the most affecting scene presented itself when they came to the place where their countrymen had been butchered: the ground was bestrewed with heads and bones of their murdered men." *

De Vries, being a prudent and humane man, made no attempt to punish the Indians, but by acts of kindness succeeded in opening a friendly intercourse with them. He ascended the Delaware as far as the site of Fort Nassau, and then pro-

---

* "Original Settlements on the Delaware," by B. Ferris.

ceeded to New Amsterdam. He attributed the failure of the Dutch settlements on the Delaware to the unjust dealings and imperious conduct of the colonists; and after an intimate acquaintance of many years with the Indian character, has left on record this testimony: "They will do no harm, if no harm is done to them."

The next attempt to plant a colony on the western bank of the Delaware was made by the Swedes in the year 1638. Peter Minuit, who commanded the expedition, had been director-general of the Dutch West India Company and governor of the New Netherlands. Being dismissed from that office, he determined to offer his services to the crown of Sweden. The officers in the expedition were mostly military men; they were provided with troops, arms and ammunition, brought with the express purpose of establishing a military post.

Although the Dutch had failed in their attempts to establish colonies on the banks of the Delaware, they still claimed the country for their government on the ground of discovery, which was then deemed sufficient by the potentates of Christendom to give them a preference in the purchase and settlement of lands inhabited by uncivilized nations. When Kieft, the governor-general of the New Netherlands, was informed of the hostile movement of the Swedes, he immediately issued a protest against the encroachment, and declared his intention to protect the rights of the Dutch to the territory invaded.*

The Swedes arrived in the spring, and sailing up Delaware Bay, they came to a promontory since called Mispillion Point, where they landed, and found the climate and the scenery so delightful after their long voyage, that they named it "Paradise Point." Embarking again, they proceeded up the Delaware to the mouth of the Minquas River, which they subsequently named Christina, in honor of the young queen of Sweden. Passing up the Minquas, they came to a point called "The Rocks," where a natural wharf of stone seemed to invite their landing, and there they disembarked and began to erect their fort.

The Dutch governor at New Amsterdam, not being supplied with the means to support his claim over the lands on the Delaware, made no attempt to prevent by force of arms the Swedish occupation, and for some years the colony they founded remained in undisturbed tranquillity, receiving fresh accessions of Scandinavian settlers.

The Dutch valued the land only for purposes of trade, and made few improvements; the Swedes were an agricultural people, and immediately

---

* "Original Settlements on the Delaware," by B. Ferris, p. 38.

began to open farms and plant fruit trees. Being mild and peaceable, their intercourse with the natives was entirely friendly, and they found no difficulty in procuring subsistence.

In the year 1642 the Swedish government sent out, under the command of John Printz, two ships of war, having on board arms, ammunition, troops, a large number of emigrants, and a clergyman. They landed a short distance above the spot where Chester now stands, and at a place called Tinicum, they built a fort and named it New Gottenburg. John Printz, lieutenant-colonel in the army, was in his commission styled governor of New Sweden. The instructions he received from his government required him to cultivate a friendly intercourse with the Dutch, "but positively to deny their *pretended* right to any part of the land on the west side of the Delaware River, purchased by the Swedes from the Indians, and to prohibit Swedish vessels passing their Fort Nassau ; and he was authorized, if all friendly negotiation proved fruitless, to *repel force by force.*" In these instructions we see the indication of a warlike policy which gave rise to contention, and eventually brought on a war with the Dutch, that put an end to the Swedish authority in America.

Printz was an energetic officer, bold, arbitrary and persevering. He fortified both shores of the

INTRODUCTION. 17

river, and when the Dutch had re-established their authority at Fort Nassau, he exacted tolls from their vessels passing up the river to visit their settlements.

In the year 1647, Peter Stuyvesant succeeded Kieft as governor of the New Netherlands, and being an energetic officer, he took active measures to counteract the aggressive movements of the Swedes on the Delaware. He caused a fort to be erected, in the year 1651, on the site now occupied by the town of New Castle, which he named Fort Cassimer. The Dutch forces on the Delaware were continually augmented, and frequent quarrels ensued between them and the Swedes, until the year 1654, when John Rysingh arrived, in a ship of war, and was invested with the government of the Swedish colony. He immediately attacked the Dutch Fort Cassimer, and the garrison being unprepared for resistance surrendered without a struggle.

Governor Stuyvesant, being informed of the loss of his fort, determined to prepare for active retaliation, but prudently concealed his purpose until the summer of 1655, when he appeared in the Delaware with a squadron of seven armed ships and transports containing between six and seven hundred men. The Swedish governor, being surprised at the appearance of an armament greatly superior to his own forces, resorted to negotiation, and protested against the evident designs of the Dutch, but Stuyvesant was not to be moved from his purpose; he demanded the surrender of the forts, and claimed possession of the territory occupied by the Swedes. Governor Rysingh, seeing that resistance would be in vain, capitulated, and the Dutch governor, after taking possession, issued a proclamation, by which all the Swedes who desired to remain in the country were required to come forward and take the oath of allegiance.

Thus terminated the Swedish dominion on the banks of the Delaware. It took the sword and perished with the sword.

It has been remarked by the historian of "The Original Settlements on the Delaware" that "it was, perhaps, one of the most fruitful sources of unhappiness to the Swedish emigrants, that their colonial rulers were always military characters, relying more on coercive power than on the omnipotent influence of justice, candor, benevolence and truth. There are few instances in the history of the human family where the disparity between the character of a people and their rulers was more apparent than in the case before us."*

The Swedish colonists were industrious and

---

* Ferris' "Original Settlements on the Delaware," p. 100.

peaceable, with strong religious feelings, and warm domestic attachments. They had lived in peace with their Indian neighbors, and after their submission to the Dutch they manifested no disposition to revolt, but quietly pursued their industrial avocations. The aggressive disposition of their military rulers, so far from protecting them, had been the source of their greatest troubles and caused the downfall of the Swedish dominion in America.

The main object of the Dutch West India Company, in extending their settlements, was to increase their trade and secure to themselves the whole commerce of the territories on the Delaware. They introduced a few more settlers, but they made little progress in the improvement of the colony.

"Under the leaden sceptre of a Dutch trading company everything beautiful, and fair, and good languished. The people were discouraged and indolent; the lands, by nature fruitful, were neglected, and lay waste. The manners of the people were rude and unpolished, education was not promoted, the standard of morals was low, and the population, which had gradually augmented under the Swedish dominion, had increased but little under that of the Dutch." *

During nine years after the conquest of the

---

* Ferris' "Original Settlements on the Delaware," p. 111.

Swedish colony the Dutch retained possession of the territory on the western bank of the Delaware, and of the country on the shores of the Hudson, then called the New Netherlands, of which New Amsterdam was the capital. The English, at the same time, occupied the rest of the North American coast from Maine to Carolina. In the year 1664, Charles II., being covetous to obtain the control of the whole coast, sent a small squadron, under the command of Colonel Nicholls and Sir Robert Carr, with instructions to reduce the Dutch forts and put the Duke of York in possession of the New Netherlands.

The English and Dutch governments were then at peace, and the governor of New Amsterdam, when the English fleet appeared, remonstrated against this unprovoked invasion, asserting that the Dutch had bought the Indian title and planted the colony fifty years before. Colonel Nicholls, regardless of the governor's remonstrance, made preparations to attack the fort, and Stuyvesant, being conscious that he could not defend it, agreed to articles of capitulation. New Amsterdam having thus fallen into the hands of the British, the rest of the New Netherlands soon submitted, and the squadron, under the command of Sir Robert Carr, proceeded to the Delaware.

On the arrival of Carr before Fort Cassimer,

INTRODUCTION. 21

"the burgomasters, on behalf of themselves and all the Dutch and Swedes," submitted without resistance, and the British authority was established.

Colonel Nicholls, on the submission of the Dutch, assumed the administration of the New Netherlands as governor, under the Duke of York, and the city, with the territory adjoining, received the name of New York.

New Jersey had been granted by the Duke of York to Lord Berkeley and Sir George Cartaret, and the territory on the west side of the Delaware remained under the control of the Duke.

In the year 1667, Governor Nicholls was succeeded by Colonel Francis Lovelace, as Governor of New York and its dependencies. His administration was arbitrary and unsatisfactory to the colonists.

In 1673, the Dutch and English being at war, a Dutch fleet, under the command of Admiral Evertsen, recaptured New York and its dependencies. Anthony Colve was appointed governor-general, and Peter Alrich, his deputy, as commandant over the territory on the Delaware. The transfer of allegiance to the Dutch government did not long continue, for a treaty was made the following year, under which the country was restored to the English. In the autumn of 1674,

Major Edward Andross arrived at New York and assumed the government, by authority from the Duke of York. All the functions of the executive and legislative departments were vested in him and his council, and their authority extended not only over New York and its dependencies on the Delaware, but also over New Jersey, although a government had been established there by an express grant from the Duke of York to the proprietors.* Among the powers claimed by Andross was that of imposing duties on exports and imports, which were levied on all vessels navigating the Delaware, whether destined to the ports of New Jersey or those on the west side of the river. This unwarrantable exaction, and other arbitrary acts of Governor Andross, gave much dissatisfaction and retarded the growth of the colonies under his control.

Let us now take a retrospective survey of the results of military rule on the banks of the Delaware. Fifty years had elapsed since the first colony was planted by the Dutch and named Fort Nassau. It languished a few years, and was, for a time, abandoned. Their next attempt was a fortified settlement near the mouth of Delaware Bay, which was destroyed by the Indians. The Swedes succeeded them and planted a colony, but

---

* Ferris' "Original Settlements on the Delaware."

INTRODUCTION.   23

the aggressive policy of their military governor brought on a war which resulted in their subjection to the Dutch. These, in turn, were conquered by the English, and the country, under the despotic sway of the governors Lovelace and Andross, made but little progress in population or industrial pursuits. Agriculture was at a low ebb, education neglected, and the moral condition of the people by no means encouraging.

There was, however, a brighter day about to dawn upon the shores of the Delaware. The colony of New Jersey was already enjoying the benefits of civil and religious liberty, the doctrine of peace and good-will to men had been proclaimed there by Penn and his associates, and the time was drawing nigh when Pennsylvania would exhibit to the world the nearest approach that has ever been made to a government founded on Christian principles.

PEACE PRINCIPLES EXEMPLIFIED

IN THE

EARLY HISTORY OF PENNSYLVANIA.

CHAPTER I.

BIRTH AND EDUCATION OF WILLIAM PENN—
SETTLEMENT OF NEW JERSEY.

1644-1678.

THE steps by which William Penn was lead to take an interest in American colonization, and the preparation he received for his great work as the founder of a commonwealth, are worthy of note, as an instance of that providential care by which the Most High directs the destinies of his chosen instruments, and accomplishes his own beneficent purposes.

He was born in London, in the year 1644, and was the son of Sir William Penn, a distinguished admiral in the English navy. He received at Oxford a liberal education, and while there became deeply impressed with religious convictions under the preaching of Thomas Loe, a minister in the Society of Friends. On his return home his father saw with grief the serious deportment of his son, which he feared would blast the prospects of worldly honor he had cherished for him. He therefore sent him to France, in company with some persons of rank who were about to make the tour of Europe. During this tour he sought the company of men distinguished for learning and piety, and returned home enriched with knowledge and polished in manners. Soon after his return he became, at his father's suggestion, a student at Lincoln's Inn, in order to acquire a knowledge of the laws of England.

In the spring of 1666, his father, having a large estate in Ireland, sent him thither, and procured him an introduction to the Lord-Lieutenant, the Duke of Ormond, who presided over a court of gayety and splendor. While residing there, he joined a military expedition sent to quell a mutiny in the garrison of Carrickfergus, and evinced so much valor and energy that the duke wished to make him a captain of infantry. This post he was desirous to obtain; for the gay world around him had in a great measure obliterated his serious impressions, and imbued him with a love of military glory.

Happily for him, his father refused his consent, and in thus frustrating the ambitious aspirations of his son, he unwittingly reserved him for a nobler field of service to which he was destined by Divine Providence.

While residing in Ireland, he went to Cork on business, where he heard that Thomas Loe was to attend a Friends' meeting in that city, and his affection for that eminent minister induced him to attend. After an interval of silent worship, Thomas Loe commenced his discourse with these words: "There is a faith which overcomes the world, and there is a faith which is overcome by the world." On this theme he spoke so impressively that the feelings of William Penn were effectually reached, his religious convictions were revived, and yielding to the operation of divine grace, he resolved to renounce the glory of the world and devote himself to the service of God.

Having become an attendant of the religious meetings of Friends, he was soon subjected to the opprobrium and persecution they everywhere endured. In the autumn of 1667, he was, with eighteen others, taken from a Friends' meeting in Cork and committed to prison. From thence he wrote a letter to the Earl of Orrery, Lord-President of Munster, in which he says, "Religion, which is at once my crime and mine innocence, makes me a prisoner to a mayor's malice, but mine own free man." In this letter he pleads for liberty of conscience, a noble principle, more fully developed in his subsequent works. It was the beginning of that long series of efforts in favor of universal toleration, which after more than twenty years of arduous conflict, were crowned with success.

His request, so far as related to himself, was granted by the earl, who gave an order for his immediate release.

The report that he had become a Quaker soon reached his father, who was induced to recall him, an order which he promptly obeyed. The admiral, seeing that his son firmly adhered to his religious principles, and his unceremonious behavior, was highly incensed, and finding remonstrance and entreaty ineffectual, expelled him from his house.

His situation was painful and embarrassing. Being destitute of pecuniary resources and without a trade or profession, he was for a time dependent on the hospitality of his friends. At length his father, softened, perhaps, by the entreaties of his wife, who was an excellent woman, allowed him to obtain subsistence at home, though he gave him no open countenance.

In the year 1668, he felt himself called to the gospel ministry, and about the same date became known as a writer of religious works. One of his earliest publications, entitled the "Sandy Foundation Shaken," gave great offence to the clergy and especially to the Bishop of London, insomuch that an order was procured for Penn's imprisonment in the tower, where he was confined with great rigor, and his friends were denied access to him.

During his imprisonment, Dr. Stillingfleet, afterwards bishop of Worcester, came at the king's request to endeavor to change his judgment; but he told the doctor, who repeated the same to the king, "That the Tower was the worst argument in the world to convince him; for whoever was in the wrong, those who used force for religion never could be in the right."

He remained a prisoner nearly nine months, and his discharge from the Tower came from the king, through the intercession of his brother, the Duke of York, who afterwards took the title of James II. This kindness on the part of the duke, and his continued favor after he became king, produced in the mind of Penn a sentiment of gratitude, and a strong personal attachment, which continued through life, and subjected him to groundless suspicion and persecution, after the fall of his royal patron.

In the year 1670, the Conventicle Act was

renewed, which was professedly against "Seditious conventicles," but really intended to suppress all religious meetings conducted "in any other manner than according to the liturgy and practice of the church of England." It was said to have been enacted at the suggestion of some of the bishops.

It was not long before Penn was made to feel the force of this arbitrary law, for on going to the meeting at Grace church street, he found the house guarded by a band of soldiers. He and other Friends, not being permitted to enter, gathered about the doors, where, after standing some time in silence, he felt it his duty to preach, but had not proceeded far when he and William Mead were arrested by the constables, who produced warrants from Sir Samuel Starling, the mayor of London.

The trial, as related in the published works of Penn, is deeply interesting, and resulted in the greater security and more firm establishment of civil liberty in England. The indictment charged that "they did unlawfully and tumultuously assemble and congregate themselves together, to the disturbance of the peace." The jury brought in a verdict of not guilty, and after being menaced and reviled by the court, they were fined forty marks each, which they refused to pay, and were committed to prison.

Penn and Mead were also fined, and imprisoned in Newgate. The jury, through their counsel, applied for redress to the court of common pleas; that tribunal overruled the decision of the lower court and set the prisoners free, which was regarded by the advocates of civil and religious liberty as a triumph of their cause.

Admiral Penn was drawing near the close of life, he longed to see his son, and sent the money privately to pay his fine and that of his companion in bonds. The meeting between the father and son was deeply moving to both, a complete reconciliation took place, and the admiral, being at last convinced of the noble character of his son, said to him, just before he died: "Son William, if you and your friends keep to your plain way of preaching and to your plain way of living, you will make an end of the priests to the end of the world. Bury me by my mother. Live in love. Shun all manner of evil, and I pray God to bless you all, and he will bless you."

Within three months from the time of his enlargement, Penn was again arrested, while preaching at a Friends' meeting, and being arraigned before Sir John Robinson, lieutenant of the Tower, he was sentenced to six months' imprisonment in Newgate. While incarcerated in this "loathsome abode of misery and crime," the pure and active mind of Penn was engaged in writing religious tracts, the most important of which is entitled, "The Great Cause of Liberty of Conscience once more briefly Debated and Defended by the Authority of Reason, Scripture, and Antiquity."

This able work, and others of a like character by the same author, exerted a powerful influence in preparing the public mind for that change of policy in regard to toleration, which he afterwards had the happiness to see adopted by the British government.

The time was now drawing nigh when Penn was to take an active and conspicuous part in the affairs of the American continent, where he was destined to carry into practice those Christian principles for which he had been pleading and suffering.

Lord Berkeley, in the year 1675, for the sum of one thousand pounds, sold his half of the province of New Jersey to John Fenwick, in trust for Edward Byllinge and his assigns. Fenwick and Byllinge, both members of the Society of Friends, became involved in a dispute about the property, and having confidence in the judgment of Penn, they agreed to refer the matter to him for arbitration. The dispute being adjusted by the kind offices of Penn, one-tenth of West New Jersey was retained by Fenwick, and the remaining nine-tenths transferred, at the request of Byllinge, to William Penn, Gawen Lawrie, and Nicholas Lucas, trustees for the benefit of his creditors.

Fenwick, in the same year, embarked with his family, and several other Friends, to take possession of the land assigned him. As the ship proceeded up the Delaware they were attracted by "a pleasant rich spot," at which they landed, and being pleased with the quietness and repose of the scene, they gave to their settlement the name of Salem. The Indians were then numerous in that neighborhood, and soon after the arrival of Fenwick, he convened the chiefs, with whom he contracted for the purchase of their right and title to the lands now included in Salem and Cumberland counties.

In the meantime the three trustees of Byllinge—Penn, Lawrie, and Lucas—sold and transferred shares in the province to a number of other Friends, who thus became joint proprietors with them.

In order to promote the settlement of West New Jersey, a constitution was drawn up by Penn and his associates, and signed by one hundred and fifty-one persons interested in the colony. This paper, dated 1676, is entitled, "Concessions and Agreements of the Proprietors, Freeholders and Inhabitants of the Province of West New Jersey." In a letter from the trustees to one of the colonists, supposed to have been written by Penn, they say:

"We have made concessions by ourselves, being such as Friends here, and there (we question not) will approve of, having sent a copy of them to James Wasse; there we lay a foundation for after ages to understand their liberty as men and Christians, that they may not be brought in bondage, but by their own consent; for *we put the power in the people;* that is to say, they to meet and choose one honest man for each propriety who hath subscribed the concessions; all these men to meet as an assembly, there to make and repeal laws, to choose a governor, or a commissioner, and twelve assistants to execute the laws during their pleasure; so every man is capable to choose or be chosen. No man to be arrested, condemned, imprisoned, or molested in his estate or liberty, but by twelve men of the neighborhood; no man to lie in prison for debt; but that his estate satisfy as far as it will go, and be set at liberty to work; no person to be called in question or molested for his conscience, or for worshipping according to his conscience; with many other things mentioned in the said concessions."

This Constitution was, doubtless, the most liberal that had then been established in any American colony.

In the years 1677 and 1678 five vessels sailed for the province of West New Jersey with eight hundred emigrants, most of whom were members of the Society of Friends. Commissioners were sent out by the proprietors, with power to buy land from the natives, and to inspect the rights of such as claimed property, to order lands laid out and to administer the government. They selected for a settlement a place called Chygoes Island; and the town they laid out was first called Beverly, afterwards Bridlington, and finally Burlington.

The colonists made it their first care on landing to establish meetings for Divine worship and Christian discipline. At the place where Burlington now stands, their first meetings were held under a tent covered with sail cloth. Here they were held regularly at stated times, until John Woolton built his house, which was the first frame house erected in Burlington.

Among the objects that first claimed the attention of their meetings for discipline, were the care and support of the poor, the orderly conduct of their members and the solemnization of marriages. In these several respects, as well as in their efforts to put an end to the traffic in ardent spirits with the natives, they faithfully followed their convictions of duty, and the colony was blessed with an unusual degree of prosperity and happiness under the government of Penn and his associates. Colonists arrived in considerable numbers, good order and harmony prevailed, the country proved to be productive, the air was salubrious, and the Indians, being treated kindly, and dealt with justly, were found to be excellent neighbors. The Friends, who had been persecuted with relentless severity in their native land, found a peaceful and happy asylum in the forests of the new world, among a people who had hitherto been reputed as ruthless savages.

In the same province, ten years before, the "Concessions" of Cartaret and Berkeley required each colonist to provide himself with a good musket, powder and balls; but now, the Friends came among their red brethren, armed only with the weapons of the Christian's warfare—integrity, benevolence, and truth; they met them without fear or suspicion; trusting in that universal principle of light and life which visits all minds, and would, if not resisted, bind the whole human family in one harmonious fraternity.

CHAPTER II.

COLONIZATION OF PENNSYLVANIA.

1680-1682.

THE progress of mankind, to a higher level of civilization and moral refinement, than was attained by the nations of antiquity, has been justly attributed to the influence of Christianity, although the holy principles of our religion have, in general, been imperfectly appreciated, and still more imperfectly carried out in practice.

In no respect has this dereliction from first principles been more disastrous, than in continuing the custom of war, which, though opposed to the doctrine and spirit of Christ, has, nevertheless, prevailed to an enormous extent among nations professing the Christian religion. In order that an example might be set up to the nations, to show how war may be avoided and its dreadful consequences averted, simply by following the precepts of Christ and trusting in Divine protection, William Penn and his associates were made the instruments of the Most High to extend the Redeemer's kingdom.

He inherited from his father, Admiral Penn, a claim on the British government for money advanced and services rendered to the amount of sixteen thousand pounds, and in the year 1680, petitioned Charles II. to grant him in lieu of this sum, a tract of country in America, lying north of Maryland, "bounded on the east by the Delaware river, on the west limited as Maryland, and northward to extend as far as plantable." *

The object of this enterprise was not only to provide a peaceful home for the persecuted members of his own Society, but to afford an asylum for the good and oppressed of every nation, and to found an empire where the pure and peaceable principles of Christianity might be exemplified in practice.

Penn's application being granted, a patent was prepared for the king's signature, which was affixed to it under date 4th of March, 1681. The name of Pennsylvania was given by the king in honor of Admiral Penn.

The preamble of the royal charter declares that William Penn's application for the territory arose out of "a commendable desire to enlarge the British empire, and promote such useful commodities

---

* Hazard's "Annals," 475.

as may be a benefit to the king and his dominions; and also to reduce the savage nations, by just and gentle manners, to the love of civil society and the Christian religion."

By the terms of the charter, William Penn is made absolute proprietary, saving to the king and his successors the sovereignty of the country and the allegiance of Penn, as well as all who shall be tenants under him. He was to acknowledge his fealty by paying to the king two beaver skins annually, and also one-fifth part of all the gold and silver ore which should be found in the province. The proprietary, with the assent and approbation of the freemen of the colony, was empowered to make all necessary laws not inconsistent with the laws of England. He was authorized to appoint magistrates and judges, to grant pardons, except for crimes of wilful murder and treason, and in these cases to grant reprieves until the king's pleasure should be known therein. The laws of the province were to be transmitted to the privy council for approbation. Penn and his heirs were to enjoy such customs on imports and exports in the province, as the people or their representatives when assembled might reasonably assess, "saving to the king and his successors such impositions and customs as are, or by *act of Parliament* shall be, appointed." This last clause conceded to Parliament the power to tax the colony, a claim which, being afterwards asserted in some of the American provinces, led to momentous consequences.

Within a month from the date of the charter, the king issued a declaration stating the grant that had been made to Penn, and requiring all persons settled in the province to yield obedience to him as absolute proprietor and governor. About the same time Penn addressed the following letter to the inhabitants of Pennsylvania:

"MY FRIENDS:—I wish you all happiness here and hereafter. These are to let you know that it hath pleased God in his providence, to cast you within my lot and care. It is a business, that, though I never undertook before, yet God hath given me an understanding of my duty, and an honest mind to do it uprightly. I hope you will not be troubled at your change and the king's choice, for you are now fixed at the mercy of no governor that comes to make his fortune great; you shall be governed by *laws of your own making*, and live a free, and if you will, a sober and industrious people. I shall not usurp the right of any, or oppress his person. God has furnished me with a better resolution, and has given me his grace to keep it. In short, whatever sober and free men can reasonably desire for the security and improvement of their own happiness, I shall heartily comply with, and in five months resolve, if it please God, to see you. In the meantime pray submit to the commands of my deputy, so far as they are consistent with the law, and pay him those dues [that formerly you paid to the order of the Governor of New York] for my use and benefit; and so I wish God to direct you in the way of righteousness, and therein prosper you and your children after you. I am your true friend,

WM. PENN.

LONDON, 8th of the month called April, 1681.

"Such," says Bancroft, "were the pledges of the Quaker sovereign on assuming the government; it is the duty of history to state, that, during his long reign, these pledges were redeemed. He never refused the free men of Pennsylvania a reasonable desire."

Penn's letter to the colonists and the king's declaration were taken out to the province by Captain William Markham, a cousin of the proprietary, who was commissioned to act as his deputy.

The concessions or conditions agreed upon in England between the proprietary and those purchasers who were to be engaged with him in the enterprise, evince an earnest desire that justice should be done to the Indians, who were then the principal owners of the soil. Goods sold to them or exchanged for furs were to be exhibited in open market, in order that imposition might be prevented, or frauds detected; no colonist was allowed to affront or wrong an Indian, without incurring the same penalty, as if committed against his fellow-planter; all differences between Indians and colonists to be settled by a jury of twelve men, six of whom should be Indians; and the natives were to have all the privileges of planting their grounds and providing for their families enjoyed by the colonists.

Penn, in a letter to one of his friends, stated that in obtaining the charter for his province he had relied upon God's favor. "I have," he says, "so obtained it, and desire that I may not be unworthy of his love, but do that which may answer his kind providence and serve his truth and people; that an example may be set up to the nations; there may be room there, though not here, for such an *holy experiment.*"

In another letter he mentioned an offer he had refused of six thousand pounds and an annual revenue for the monopoly of the Indian trade between the Delaware and Susquehanna. "I will not abuse the love of God," he wrote, "nor act unworthy of his providence, and so defile what came to me clean. No; let the Lord guide me by his wisdom and preserve me to honor his name, and serve his truth and people, that an example and standard may be set up to the nations; there may be room there, though not here."

In the autumn of 1681, three commissioners were appointed by the proprietary, with instructions to proceed to the colony, make arrangements for a settlement, lay out a town, and treat with the Indians.

The following letter to the Indians was intrusted to the commissioners:

"LONDON, 18th of 8th month, 1681.

"MY FRIENDS :—There is one great God and power that hath made the world and all things therein, to whom you and I, and all people, owe their being and well-being, and to whom you and I must one day give an account for all that we have done in the world.

"This great God has written his laws in our hearts, by which we are taught and commanded to love and to help and to do good to one another. Now, this great God hath been pleased to make me concerned in your part of the world, and the king of the country where I live hath given me a great province therein, but I desire to enjoy it with your love and consent, that we may always live together as neighbors and friends, else what would the great God do to us who hath made us (not to devour and destroy one another, but) to live soberly and kindly together in the world? Now, I would have you well observe that I am very sensible of the unkindness and injustice which have been too much exercised towards you by the people of these parts of the world, who have sought themselves to make great advantages by you, rather than be examples of justice and goodness unto you. This I hear hath been a matter of trouble to you, and caused great grudging and animosities, sometimes to the shedding of blood, which hath made the great God angry. But I am not such a man, as is well known in my own country. I have great love and regard toward you, and desire to win and gain your love and friendship by a kind, just and peaceable life, and the people I send are of the same mind; and shall in all things behave themselves accordingly, and if in anything any shall offend you or your people, you shall have a full and speedy satisfaction for the same by an equal number of just men on both sides, that by no means you may have just occasion of being offended against them.

"I shall shortly come to see you myself, at which time we may more largely and freely confer and discourse of these matters. In the mean time I have sent my commissioners to treat with you about land and a firm league of peace. Let me desire you to be kind to them and to the people, and receive the presents and tokens which I have sent you as a testimony of my good-will to you, and of my resolution to live justly, peaceably and friendly with you.

"I am your loving friend,

"WILLIAM PENN."

The commissioners, with other emigrants, sailed in the autumn of 1681, and arrived at Upland (now called Chester) in the winter. They were well provided with stores, and the colonists already there treated them with hospitality.

The population of the province, exclusive of Indians, was then about two thousand souls, consisting mostly of Swedes and English, whose habitations were scattered along the western bank of the Delaware.

The first constitution or frame of government agreed upon in England between the proprietary and others concerned in the first settlement is dated 25th of April, 1682. It was published the following month, accompanied by a preface explanatory of the general principles of government.

In this admirable paper he shows that civil government has been ordained by Divine Providence chiefly for two ends: " First, to terrify evil doers; secondly, to cherish those that do well.". . . "They weakly err," he says, " who think there is no other use of government than correction, which is the coarsest part of it. Daily experience tells us, that the care and regulation of many other affairs, more soft and daily necessary, make up much the greatest part of government, and which must have followed the peopling of the world, had Adam never fallen, and will continue among men on earth under the highest attainments they may arrive at by the coming of the blessed second Adam, the Lord from heaven.". . . " I do not find a model in the world, that time, place, and some singular emergencies have not necessarily altered; nor is it easy to frame a civil government that shall serve all places alike. I know what is said by the several admirers of monarchy, aristocracy and democracy, which are the rule of one, of a few, and of many, and are the three common ideas of government when men discourse on that subject. But I choose to solve the controversy with this small distinction, and it belongs to all three: any government is free to the people under it, whatever be the frame, where the laws rule and the people are a party to those laws; and more than this is tyranny, oligarchy or confusion."

"Governments rather depend upon men, than men upon governments. Let men be good and the government cannot be bad. If it be ill, they will cure it. But if men be bad, let the government be ever so good, they will endeavor to warp and spoil it to their turn. I know some say: Let us have good laws and no matter for the men that execute them. But let them consider, that though good laws do well, good men do better; for good laws may want good men, and be abolished or evaded by evil men; but good men will never want good laws, nor suffer ill ones."...."That therefore which makes a good constitution must keep it, namely, men of wisdom and virtue, qualities that, because they descend not with worldly inheritances, must be carefully propagated by a virtuous education of youth, for which after ages will owe more to the care and prudence of founders and the successive magistracy, than to their parents for their private patrimonies."

"We have, with reverence to God and good conscience to men, to the best of our skill contrived and composed the frame and laws of this government to the great end of all government, viz., to support power in reverence with the people, and to secure the people from the abuse of power, that they may be free by their just obedience, and the magistrates honorable for their just administration;

for liberty without obedience is confusion, and obedience without liberty is slavery."

The constitution agreed upon in England, and intended to be submitted for acceptance or modification, to the colonists in Pennsylvania, was liberal beyond any frame of government then existing. It placed the legislative and judicial departments in the hands of the people, who were to elect by ballot their representatives in the council and general assembly. The executive alone was hereditary, in conformity with the provisions of the royal charter.

The territory on Delaware Bay, which now constitutes the State of Delaware, had been granted by the king Charles II. to his brother James, Duke of York. After much negotiation, Penn obtained from the Duke two deeds of feoffment, by one of which he conveyed the town of New Castle and the country lying within a circle of twelve miles around it, and by the other he conveyed all the land on Delaware Bay from twelve miles south of New Castle to Cape Henlopen. For the first he was to pay the Duke the yearly rent of five shillings, and for the second "one rose at the feast of St. Michael the Archangel yearly, if demanded," together with a moiety of all rents and profits thereof.

In the year 1681, Penn became interested in

the property and government of East New Jersey, of which Elizabethtown was the capital. Sir George Cartaret, the former proprietary of this province, having died, it was sold under his will to pay his debts, and Penn became the purchaser on behalf of himself and eleven other persons. The twelve proprietaries soon after admitted twelve others, and to these twenty-four proprietaries the Duke of York made a fresh grant of East New Jersey in the year 1682. They instituted a government called the Council of Proprietaries, whose meetings were held twice in the year at Perth-Amboy.

William Penn, having made all his arrangements for a passage to Pennsylvania, embarked on the ship Welcome of 300 tons burthen, Robert Greenway, master. On the eve of his departure, he addressed a beautiful letter to his wife and children, replete with instruction on their temporal affairs and spiritual welfare. In relation to his American possessions he says to his children: "As for you who are likely to be concerned in the government of Pennsylvania and my parts of East Jersey, especially the first, I do charge you before the Lord God and his holy angels that you be lowly, diligent and tender, fearing God, loving the people and hating covetousness. Let justice have its impartial course, and the laws free passage.

Though to your loss, protect no man against it; for you are not above the law, but the law above you. Live, therefore, the lives yourselves you would have the people live, and then you have right and boldness to punish the transgressor. Keep upon the square, for God sees you: therefore do your duty, and be sure you see with your own eyes, and hear with your own ears. Entertain no lurchers, cherish no informers for gain or revenge; use no tricks; fly to no devices to support or cover injustice, but let your hearts be upright before the Lord, trusting in him above the contrivances of men, and none shall be able to hurt or supplant."

On the 27th of October, 1682, the ship Welcome arrived at New Castle, where William Penn and his fellow-passengers were joyfully welcomed by the inhabitants. On the 28th he met the people at the court-house, when he made a speech to the old magistrates, in which he explained to them the design of his coming, the nature and end of government, and of that more particularly which he came to establish.

The next day he was at Upland, accompanied by a number of his friends. Addressing his friend Pearson, he said: "Providence has brought us here safe. Thou hast been the companion of my perils. What wilt thou that I should call this place?" Pearson said, "Chester" in remembrance of the city whence he came. Penn replied that it should be called Chester, and that when he divided the counties one of them should be called by the same name.

Tradition relates that from Chester to Philadelphiá he went with some of his friends in an open boat or barge, and we can readily imagine how delighted he must have been while passing up the noble Delaware, beholding its banks shaded with majestic forests clad in all the varied foliage of autumn, its surface covered with wild fowl, and everything around indicating a solitude and grandeur peculiar to the new world. After passing four miles above the mouth of the Schuylkill, they came to a place called Coaquannock, where there was a high bold shore covered with lofty pines. Here the site of the infant city of Philadelphia had been established, and we may be assured his approach was hailed with joy by the whole population; the old inhabitants, Swedes and Dutch, eager to catch a glimpse of their future governor, and the Friends who had gone before him anxiously waiting his arrival.

There is a tradition connected with his arrival which is thus related by Watson: "The Indians as well as the whites had severally prepared the best entertainment the place and circumstances could admit. William Penn made himself endeared to the Indians by his marked condescension and acquiescence in their wishes. He walked with them, sat with them on the ground, and ate with them of their roasted acorns and hominy.

At this they expressed their great delight and soon began to show how they could hop and jump; at which exhibition, William Penn, to cap the climax, sprang up and beat them all.

We are not prepared to credit such light gayety in a sage governor and religious chief; but we have the positive assertion of a woman of truth, who says she saw it. There may have been very wise policy in the measure as an act of conciliation, worth more than a regiment of sharpshooters. He was sufficiently young for any agility, and we remember that one of the old journalists among the Friends incidentally speaks of him as having naturally an excess of levity of spirit for a grave minister.

The site of Philadelphia had been determined by the commissioners, in conformity with the proprietary's instruction, before his arrival, and some progress had been made in laying out the streets and building houses. Penn was well pleased with the location. In describing it he wrote as follows: "The situation is a neck of land, and lieth between two navigable rivers, Delaware and

Schuylkill, whereby it hath two fronts upon the water, each a mile, and two from river to river. Delaware is a glorious river; but the Schuylkill, being an hundred miles boatable above the falls, and its course northeast toward the fountain of the Susquehannah (that tends to the heart of the province and both sides our own), it is like to be a great part of the settlement of this age." . . . "This I will say for the good providence of God, that of all the many places I have seen in the world, I remember not one better seated; so that it seems to me to have been appointed for a town, whether we regard the rivers or the conveniency of the coves, docks and springs, the loftiness and soundness of the land and the air, held by the people of those parts to be very good."

Several changes were made in the location and names of the streets after Governor Penn's arrival. Broad street, which is parallel with the Delaware, and lies nearly midway between that river and the Schuylkill, had not been located on the highest ground, and the governor had it changed to the top of the ridge, though nearer the Schuylkill, so that the public buildings intended to be placed there should overlook the whole city. Many of the streets had been named after prominent individuals among the colonists; for instance, what is now Walnut was first called

Pool street, Mulberry was Holmes street, Chestnut was Union street, etc., which not being satisfactory to the proprietary, he gave the name of High street to the wide central avenue leading from river to river, and the main streets parallel with it he called after the names of forest trees found there. The cross streets were named according to their numbers, as Front, Second, Third, etc., beginning at each river and counting to Broad street.* He reserved in the middle of the city, at the intersection of High and Broad streets, a large square for public buildings, and for health and recreation, and in each of the four divisions of the city was a square for public walks. It was his intention and original plan not to permit buildings to be erected on the bank of the Delaware, but to have there a wide promenade the whole length of the city. This beautiful and salutary arrangement was, in after years, allowed to be infringed, and hence the crowded and irregular streets that deform the eastern front of the city.

After a brief sojourn in Philadelphia and attending some meetings of Friends, Penn went to New York "to pay his duty to the Duke of York

---

* Within a few years the names of the cross streets west of Broad have been changed, so that the numbers from that point are consecutive, to the Schuylkill.

by visiting his province." Returning through East and West Jersey, he reached Pennsylvania near the end of November, then the ninth month. It is believed that about this time he held the treaty of amity with the Indians which has been so widely celebrated as the "Great Treaty under the Elm tree at Kensington."

It is to be regretted that no circumstantial account of this treaty is found in any contemporary record. An able memoir by Peter S. Duponceau and J. Francis Fisher, presented to the Historical Society of Pennsylvania, and published in their third volume, part II., gives by far the best account of this transaction that is now extant. The place of meeting has, with much unanimity, been fixed at Shackamaxon, now called Kensington. It appears by ancient records that the name of this place was then written Sachamaxing, which signifies the place of kings, being derived from Sakima, which in the Delaware language means a king or chief. At least three Indian tribes were present: the Lenni Lenape, living near the banks of the Delaware, the Mingoes, a tribe sprung from the Iroquois and settled at Conestogo, and the Shawnese, a southern tribe that had removed to the Susquehanna. There is reason to suppose that Governor Penn would be accompanied, as usual, by some members of his council as well as his secretary and surveyor. Tradition relates that a number of prominent Friends were present, among whom was an ancestor of Benjamin West, whose portrait is introduced by the artist into his celebrated painting of the treaty scene. We must not take our idea of Penn's appearance from West's picture, in which he is represented as a corpulent old man, for at that time he was in the prime of life, being only thirty-eight years of age, robust and active, graceful in person and pleasing in manners.

His favorite mode of travelling was by water. He kept a barge furnished with a sail, and manned by a boatswain, a cockswain and six oarsmen. His mansion at Pennsbury Manor was then being built; it was near the Friends' settlement at the Falls and opposite Bordentown. Keeping in view these data, the scene may be imagined: Under the wide branching elm the Indian tribes are assembled, but all unarmed, for no warlike weapon is allowed to disturb the scene. In front are the chiefs, with their counsellors and aged men on either hand. Behind them, in the form of a half moon, sit the young men and some of the aged matrons, while beyond, and disposed in still widening circles, are seen the youth of both sexes. Among the assembled chiefs there is one who holds a conspicuous rank: the great Sachem Tam-

Peace Principles Exemplified. 57

inend, one of Nature's noblemen, revered for his wisdom and beloved for his goodness.

Turning to the river, a barge is seen approaching, bearing at its mast-head the broad pennant of the governor. The oars are plied with measured strokes, and near the helm sits William Penn, attended by his council. Among them are Markham, his secretary, Holme, surveyor-general, Simcox, Haigue, Taylor and Pearson. On the river bank, waiting with others to join them, is Lacy Cock, the hospitable Swede, whose dwelling is near the treaty ground.

They pause when they approach the council fire. Taminend puts on his chaplet, surmounted by a small horn, the emblem of kingly power; and then, through an interpreter, he announces to William Penn that the nations are ready to hear him.

Being thus called upon he begins his speech. "The Great Spirit," he says, "who made me and you, who rules the heavens and the earth, and who knows the innermost thoughts of men, knows that I and my friends have a hearty desire to live in peace and friendship with you, and to serve you to the utmost of our power. It is not our custom to use hostile weapons against our fellow-creatures, for which reason we have come unarmed. Our object is not to do injury, and thus provoke the Great Spirit, but to do good.

"We are met on the broad pathway of good faith and good will, so that no advantage is to be taken on either side, but all to be openness, brotherhood and love." Here the governor unrolls a parchment containing stipulations for trade and promises of friendship which, by means of an interpreter, he explains to them, article by article, and placing it on the ground, he observes that the ground shall be common to both people. He then proceeds: "I will not do as the Marylanders did, that is, call you children or brothers only, for parents are apt to whip their children too severely and brothers sometimes will differ, neither will I compare the friendship between us to a chain, for the rain may rust it, or a tree may fall and break it; but I will consider you as the same flesh and blood with the Christians, and the same as if one man's body were to be divided into two parts."

This speech being listened to by the Indians in perfect silence and with much gravity, they take some time to deliberate, and then the king orders one of his chiefs to speak to William Penn. The Indian orator advances, and in the king's name salutes him; then, taking him by the hand, he makes a speech pledging kindness and good neighborhood, and that the Indians and English must live in love as long as the sun and moon shall endure.

There is evidence to show that the stipulations of this treaty or league of amity were committed to writing, but the record has been sought without success. We have, however, the principal items or links of the chain as mentioned by Governor Gordon in a speech he made to the same tribes in the year 1728. He said:

"My friends and brethren, you are sensible that the great William Penn, the father of this country, when he first brought the people with him over the broad sea, took all the Indians, the old inhabitants, by the hand, and because he found them to be a sincere, honest people, he took them to his heart and loved them as his own. He then made a strong league and chain of friendship with them, by which it was agreed that the Indians and the English, with all Christians, should be as one people. Your friend and father, William Penn, still retained a warm affection for all the Indians, and strictly commanded those whom he sent to govern his people to treat the Indians as his children, and continued in this love for them until his death. . . .

"I am now to discourse with my brethren, the Conestogoes, Delawares, Ganawese and Shawnese Indians, upon the Susquehanna:

"My brethren: You have been faithful to your leagues with us, your hearts have been clean, and you have preserved the chain from spots or rust, or if there were any, you have been careful to wipe them away. Your leagues with your father, William Penn, and with his governors, are in writing on record, that our children and our children's children may have them in everlasting remembrance. And we know that you preserve the memory of those things among you by telling them to your children, and they again to the next generation, so that they remain stamped on your minds never to be forgot.

"The chief heads or strongest links of the chain I find are these nine, viz.:

"1. That all William Penn's people or Christians and all the Indians should be brethren, as the children of one father, joined together with one heart, one head and one body.

"2. That all paths should be open and free to both Christians and Indians.

"3. That the doors of the Christians' houses should be open to the Indians, and the houses of the Indians open to the Christians, and that they should make each other welcome as their friends.

"4. That the Christians should not believe any false rumors or reports of the Iñdians, nor the Indians believe any such rumors or reports of Christians, but should first come as brethren to inquire of each other; and that both Christians and Indians, when they have any such false reports of their brethren, they should bury them as in a bottomless pit.

"5. That if the Christians heard any ill news that may be to the hurt of the Indians, or the Indians heard any such ill news that may be to the injury of the Christians, they should acquaint each other with it speedily as true friends and brethren.

"6. That the Indians should do no manner of harm to the Christians nor to their creatures, nor the Christians do any hurt to the Indians, but each treat the other as brethren.

"7. But as there are wicked people in all nations, if either Indians or Christians should do any harm to each other, complaint should be made of it by the persons suffering, that right may be done; and when satisfaction is made, the injury or wrong should be forgot and be buried as in a bottomless pit.

"8. That the Indians should in all things assist the Christians, and the Christians assist the Indians against all wicked people that would disturb them.

"9. And lastly, that both Indians and Christians should acquaint their children with this league and firm chain of friendship made between them, and that it should always be made stronger and stronger, and be kept bright and clean, without rust or spot, between our children and children's children, while the creeks and rivers run, and while the sun, moon and stars endure."

It may be asked why this treaty should have inspired so much interest as to make "its fame co-extensive with the civilized world?" The pre-eminent importance of the "great treaty" consists in this: it was the first time William Penn met the Indian chiefs in council, to make with them the firm league of friendship, which was never violated, and gave rise to a kindly intercourse between the Friends and the aborigines that continues to this day. It was like laying the corner stone of a great edifice, whose enduring strength and beautiful proportions have called forth the admiration of succeeding ages.

The whole conduct of Penn toward the Indians was founded in justice and love; he not only paid them for their lands, but he employed every means in his power to promote their happiness and moral improvement. The Indians, on their part, treated the colonists in the most hospitable manner, supplying them frequently with venison, beans and maize, and refusing compensation. For William Penn they felt and often expressed the utmost confidence and esteem. So great was the reverence inspired by his virtues, that his name was embalmed in their affections and handed down to succeeding generations.

At a treaty held at Easton, in Pennsylvania, with the Indians, in 1756, in Governor Morris's administration, Teedyuscung, the Delaware chief, spoke as follows: " Brother Onas and the people of Pennsylvania, we rejoice to hear from you that you are willing to renew the old good understanding, and that you call to mind the first treaties of friendship made by Onas, our great friend, deceased, with our forefathers, when himself and his people first came over here."

The name of Onas was given to William Penn by the Iroquois, whom the proprietary, and generally the English, supported in their claim of superiority over the other Indian tribes. It seems that the Delawares adopted the name at least in their public speeches. Among themselves they called him, in their own language, Miquon. Both these words signify a quill or pen.

It is certain that no other man ever attained so great an influence over their minds; and the affectionate intercourse between them and the inhabitants of Pennsylvania, which continued as long as the principles of the first colonists preserved their ascendency, is the most beautiful exemplification afforded by history that the peaceable doctrines of Christ are adapted to secure the happiness of man.

In the other colonies the aborigines were considered as dangerous neighbors, inured to cruelty and delighting in blood. They had been rendered suspicious by the repeated injuries of the whites, and were undoubtedly brave and revengeful. Penn and his associates, relying on the purity of their motives and the protection of Divine Providence, came among them unarmed, professing the principle of non-resistance. The justice of his measures and the kindness of his deportment won their confidence and esteem; the blood-stained tomahawk was buried, the tokens of peace were exchanged, and the ferocity of their nature was subdued by the tender. cementing influence of Christian love.

CHAPTER III.

LEGISLATION AND INTERCOURSE WITH INDIANS.

1682-1683.

IN conformity with a summons from Governor Penn, a general assembly of representatives from the several counties met at Chester, on the 4th of December, 1682. They chose Nicholas Moore for their speaker, and proceeded to deliberate on the constitution and laws agreed upon in England, and submitted for their consideration.

A petition was presented from the inhabitants of the three lower counties, which now constitute the State of Delaware, " humbly desiring that they may be favored with an act of union by the governor and assembly, for their incorporation with the province of Pennsylvania, in order to the enjoyment of all the rights and privileges of that province." The petition was granted, and an act of union passed which also provided for the naturalization of foreigners already settled in the province and territories. This act being approved by the governor, the Swedes deputed Lacy Cock to acquaint him that they would love, serve and obey him with all they had, declaring "it was the best day they ever saw."

An act of settlement was passed at the same time, which states that owing to the "fewness of the inhabitants, their inability in estate, and unskilfulness in matters of government, three persons out of each of the six counties shall serve for a provincial council, and nine from each county for members of the assembly."

In the same act some other changes in the constitution are provided for, but its main features and essential principles, as agreed upon in England, are preserved, and the humble acknowledgments of the assembly are expressed for it, with a promise that it shall be universally observed.

At this session was passed the "Great Law," or code of laws, consisting of sixty-nine sections, which long formed the basis of jurisprudence in Pennsylvania. It embraces most of the laws agreed upon in England and some others afterwards suggested. Among the latter is a clause, attributed to the proprietary, requiring the estates of intestates to go to the wife and children, which, by abrogating the English law of primogeniture, was instrumental in promoting that general equality of condition and division of property deemed so essential in a republican government. The first section of this code, being a noble testimony to religious liberty, is here inserted entire:

"Almighty God being the only Lord of conscience, Father of lights and spirits, and the Author, as well as object, of all Divine knowledge, faith and worship; who only can enlighten the mind, and persuade and convince the understanding of people in due reverence to his sovereignty over the souls of mankind : It is enacted by the authority aforesaid, that no person now, or at any time hereafter, living in this province, who shall confess and acknowledge one Almighty God to be the Creator, upholder and ruler of the world, and that professeth him or herself obliged in conscience to live peaceably and justly under the civil government, shall in anywise be molested or prejudiced for his or her conscientious persuasion or practice; nor shall he or she at any time be compelled to frequent or maintain any religious worship, place or ministry whatever, contrary to his or her mind, but shall freely and fully enjoy his or her Christian liberty in that respect without any interruption or reflection ; and if any person shall abuse or deride any other for his or her different persuasion and practice in matter of religion, such shall be looked upon as a disturber of the peace, and be punished accordingly.

"But to the end that looseness, irreligion and atheism may not creep in under pretence of conscience, in this province: Be it further enacted by the authority aforesaid, that according to the good example of the primitive Christians, and for the ease of the creation, every first day of the week, called the Lord's Day, people shall abstain from their common toil and labor, that whether masters, parents, children, or servants, they may the better dispose themselves to read the Scriptures of truth, at home, or to frequent such meetings of religious worship abroad as may best suit their respective persuasions."

After a session of four days, the assembly adjourned, affording an example of unanimity and despatch almost unexampled.

According to the code of laws adopted by the general assembly, every man liable to civil burdens possessed the right of suffrage, and every Christian was eligible to office. No judicial oaths were required; no tax or custom could be levied without authority of law. Stage-plays, bull-baits and cock-fights were prohibited. Murder was the only crime punishable by death. Selling spirituous liquors to Indians to be punished by a fine of five pounds for every offence. All prisons to be workhouses for persons convicted of crime.

The laws were to be published and to be one of the books read in the schools.

The penal code, enacted by the colonists of Pennsylvania, was, in its humane provisions, far in advance of the age. Although by the charter the laws were subject to repeal when not consistent with the laws of England, they ventured to abolish, almost entirely, her sanguinary code, reserving the penalty of death for wilful murder only. It must be admitted, that even in this case, capital punishment was contrary to the principles of Friends, but perhaps the change they effected was as great as their dependent condition would allow, and, we have reason to believe, that the death-penalty was not inflicted. "Penn looked upon reformation as the great end of retributive justice."

. . "In pursuance of this idea he exempted from the infliction of death about two hundred offences which were capitally punished by the English law." * The sentiment expressed in his laws that every prison should be a work-house, and the humane regulations established for jails, gave rise to a new mode of punitive justice, the penitentiary system, in which Pennsylvania has taken the lead.

A mild code of laws vigorously executed is the true policy of nations; for it is not the severity but the certainty of punishment that deters from

---

* J. R. Tyson's address on the 200th anniversary of the birth of Penn.

the commission of crime. To provide the means of a good education for every child, and to see that all are taught some useful trade or profession, would do more for the promotion of peace and happiness than all the machinery of courts and prisons.

When we take into view that Penn's constitution was then unparalleled for its excellence, and that he ever showed a willingness to alter it in accordance with the wants and capacities of the people, we shall find few if any other legislators in ancient or modern times who so richly merit the gratitude of posterity.

"In the early constitutions of Pennsylvania are to be found the distinct annunciation of every great principle; the germ, if not the development, of every valuable improvement in government or legislation, which has been introduced into the political systems of more modern epochs." *

On the 10th of the first month (March), 1683, Penn met the provincial council at Philadelphia, and the assembly two days afterward. The council consisted of three members from each of the six counties, and the assembly of nine members from each county, agreeably to "the act of settlement," passed at the first session; but some doubts having arisen about the constitutionality of this mode of

---

* J. I. Wharton, "Watson's Annals," I., 314.

reducing the number of representatives, a member of the assembly moved, "That the governor may be desired that this alteration may not hinder the people from the benefit of the charter." The governor answered that "they might amend, alter or add for the public good, and that he was ready to settle such foundations as might be for their happiness and the good of their posterity, according to the powers vested in him."

On the 20th, the governor and council desired a conference with the assembly about the charter, and then the question being asked by the governor, whether they would have the old charter or a new one, they unanimously desired that there might be a new one, with the amendment put into a law. A joint committee of the two houses was appointed to draft a new charter, which being done, it was read in council, and after some debate it was agreed to and signed by the governor, to whom the old charter was returned, with "the hearty thanks of the whole house."

The second charter embraced the same principles as the first, and much of it was in the same language; the number of delegates from each county was reduced to three for the council, and six for the assembly, with the privilege of each house being enlarged with the increase of inhabitants. The governor's treble vote was abolished, but the privilege of originating bills was still confined to the governor and council, who were required to publish the proposed bills before the meeting of the assembly. This feature was well adapted to the circumstances of an infant colony, as it saved much time in legislation, but it was subsequently changed, with the consent of the proprietary, by giving to the assembly, at their request, power to originate all legislative measures.

By one of the acts passed at this time, provision was made for the appointment, at every county court, of three peace-makers, in the nature of common arbitrators, to hear and determine all differences between individuals.

In grateful acknowledgment of the governor's services, and in consideration of his expenses in establishing the colony, the assembly granted him an impost upon certain imports and exports; but he, with a generosity which he had afterward cause to repent, declined to avail himself of it for the present.

After an harmonious session of twenty-one days, the assembly adjourned, having in this brief time not only amended the constitution and enacted many new laws, but revised and confirmed the whole civil and criminal code.

In the year 1683 Penn negotiated with the Indians for the purchase of lands, and there are on

PEACE PRINCIPLES EXEMPLIFIED. 73

record two deeds of that date from Indian chiefs for the confirmation of such sales.

In one of the purchases of land made from the Indians it was stipulated that it should extend "as far back as a man could walk in three days." Tradition relates that William Penn himself, with several of his friends and a number of Indian chiefs, "began to walk out this land at the mouth of the Neshaminy, and walked up the Delaware, that in one day and a half they got to a spruce tree near the mouth of Baker's creek," when Penn concluding this would include as much land as he would want at present, a line was run and marked from the spruce tree to Neshaminy, and the remainder left to be walked out when it should be wanted for settlement. "It is said they walked leisurely, after the Indian manner, sitting down sometimes to smoke their pipes, to eat biscuit and cheese and drink a bottle of wine. It is certain they arrived at the spruce tree in a day and a half, the whole distance rather less than thirty miles."

The remainder of the line was not run till the 20th of September, 1733, when the governor of Pennsylvania employed three of the fastest walkers that could be found, one of whom, Edward Marshall, walked in a day and a half the astonishing distance of eighty-six miles. The name of William Penn has by some persons been unjustly coupled with this disgraceful transaction, which did not take place till many years after his death. The Indians felt themselves much aggrieved by this unfair admeasurement of their lands; it was the cause of the first dissatisfaction between them and the people of Pennsylvania, and it is remarkable that the first murder committed by them in the province, seventy-two years after the landing of Penn, was on this very ground which had been taken from them by fraud.

During the year 1683 the provincial council held its meetings in Philadelphia; it was convened very frequently, and the minutes show that William Penn always presided.

Among its judicial proceedings was a trial for witchcraft, the only one on the records. This appears to have originated among the Swedes, who probably brought with them from their native land some of the Scandinavian superstitions. The persons accused were Margaret Mattson and Yeshro Hendrickson. Lacy Cock acted as interpreter between them and the governor. The following is a sample of the testimony: Henry Drystreet, attested, saith, "he was told twenty years ago, that the prisoner at the bar was a witch, and that several cows were bewitched by her." Annaky Coolin, attested, saith, "that her husband took the heart of a calf, that had died as they thought by witchcraft, and boiled it, whereupon the prisoner at the bar came in and asked them what they were doing; they said boiling of flesh; she said they had better have boiled the bones, with several other unseemly expressions." The governor gave the jury their charge, of which, it is to be regretted, there is no record. "The jury went forth, and upon their return brought her in guilty of the common fame of being a witch, but not guilty in manner and form as she stands indicted."

This verdict probably gave a quietus to all accusations of witchcraft, which in that day were believed by many and in Massachusetts had led to melancholy results.

In the year of Penn's arrival and during the two years next succeeding, ships with emigrants arrived from London, Bristol, Ireland, Wales, Cheshire, Lancashire, Holland and Germany to the number of fifty sail. "The news spread abroad," says Bancroft, "that William Penn, the Quaker, had opened an asylum to the good and the oppressed of every nation, and humanity went through Europe gathering the children of misfortune. . . . There is nothing in the history of the human race like the confidence which the simple virtues and institutions of William Penn inspired."

The progress of the colony in population was remarkably rapid, and the fruits of industry soon became everywhere apparent. In three years from its foundation Philadelphia gained more than New York had done in half a century.

The colonists, in their native land, had been mostly husbandmen, tradesmen and mechanics. Among them were some good scholars, but generally their education was limited, and their manners were simple, hearty and unceremonious. Many of them had good estates, and were well provided with all the comforts that could be had in a new country. Some brought with them frames of houses ready to be set up, others built cabins of logs and covered them with clapboards. Huts covered with bark and turf were made to shelter them while building their houses, and excavations made in the bank of the Delaware at Philadelphia, called caves, served for temporary dwellings of the poorer class.

A large proportion of the colonists being members of the Society of Friends, their first care was to establish meetings for worship and discipline. In a letter from Friends in Pennsylvania to their brethren in Great Britain, written in 1683, they mention three meetings for worship in Bucks county, two in Philadelphia county and four in Chester county. They had three monthly meetings for discipline, and expected soon to have a yearly meeting. As to their temporal condition they say, "Blessed be God, we are satisfied; our lot is fallen every way in a goodly place, and the love of God is and growing among us, and we are a family at peace among ourselves, and truly great is our joy therefor."

Fowl, fish and venison were plenty. The wild pigeons came in such numbers that the air was sometimes darkened by their flight; and flying low, those who had no other means to take them sometimes supplied themselves by throwing at them as they flew, and salted up what they could not eat.

The Indians were remarkably kind to the colonists, supplying them with such provisions as they could spare, and were otherwise serviceable in many respects.

"John Chapman, having settled in the woods the farthest back of any English inhabitants, found the Indians very kind to his family, as well as to the other settlers that came after him, often supplying them with corn and other provisions. His twin sons, Abraham and Joseph Chapman, then about nine or ten years old, going out one evening to seek their cattle, met an Indian in the woods, who told them to go back or they would be lost. Soon after this they took his advice and went back, but it was within night before they got home, where they found the Indian, who being careful lest they should lose themselves, had repaired thither in the night to see. And their parents about that time going to the yearly meeting at Philadelphia and leaving a young family at home, the Indians came every day to see whether there was anything amiss among them."*

In the spring or summer of 1683 William Penn made a journey to the interior of his province, during which he made himself more fully acquainted with its surface, soil and natural productions, and he visited the Indians in their wigwams, with whom he learned to converse in their own language.

The result of his observations was communicated in a very interesting letter to the Free Society of Traders.†

He found the climate, soil and natural productions very satisfactory. The fruits he found in the woods were the white and black mulberry, chestnut, walnut, plums, strawberries, cranberries, hurtleberries and grapes of divers sorts.

---

* "Smith's History of Pennsylvania," and "Proud's History of Pennsylvania."
† See the Letter in "Janney's Life of William Penn."

"Peaches," he says, "are in great quantities; not an Indian plantation without them; but whether naturally here at first I know not. The woods are adorned with lovely flowers, for color, greatness, figure and variety."

His account of the Indians relates to their persons, language, manners, religion and government, with conjectures concerning their origin. The limits of this work will only allow the selection of a few passages.

"For their persons, they are generally tall, straight, well-built, and of singular proportion. They tread strong and clever, and mostly walk with a lofty chin." . . . "They grease themselves with bear's fat clarified, and using no defence against sun and weather their skins must needs be swarthy."

"Their language is lofty, yet narrow, but like the Hebrew in signification, full. Like shorthand in writing, one word serveth in the place of three, and the rest are supplied by the understanding of the hearer. Imperfect in their tenses, wanting in their moods, participles, adverbs, conjunctions, interjections. I have made it my business to understand it that I might not want an interpreter on any occasion, and I must say that I know not a language spoken in Europe that hath words of more sweetness or greatness in accent and emphasis than theirs."

"In liberality they excel. Nothing is too good for their friend. Give them a fine gun, coat or other thing, it may pass twenty hands before it sticks; light of heart, strong affections, but soon spent; the most merry creatures that live. They feast and dance perpetually; they never have much, nor want much. Wealth circulateth like blood. All parts partake; and though none shall want what another hath, yet exact observers of property. Some kings have sold, others presented me with several parcels of land. The pay or presents I made them were not hoarded by the particular owners, but the neighboring kings and their clans being present when the goods were brought out, the parties chiefly concerned consulted what and to whom they should give them. To every king then, by the hands of a person for that work appointed, is a proportion sent, so sorted and folded, and with that gravity which is admirable. Then that king subdivided it in like manner among his dependents, they hardly leaving themselves an equal share with one of their subjects; and be it on such occasions as festivals, or at their common meals, the kings distribute, and to themselves last."

"They eat twice a day, morning and evening; their seats and table are the ground. Since the Europeans came into these parts, they are grown great lovers of strong liquors, rum especially, and for it exchange the richest of their skins and furs. If they are heated with liquor, they are restless till they have enough to sleep. That is their cry, 'Some more, and I will go to sleep;' but when drunk, one of the most wretched spectacles in the world."

"These poor people are under a dark night in things relating to religion; to be sure the tradition of it, yet they believe a God and immortality without the help of metaphysics; for they say there is a great king that made them who dwells in a glorious country to the southward of them, and that the souls of the good shall go thither, where they shall live again."

"Their government is by kings, which they call sachama, and these by succession, but always on the mother's side. For instance, the children of him who is now king will not succeed, but his brother by the mother, or the children of his sister, whose sons (and after them the children of her daughters) will reign, for no woman inherits. Every king hath his council, and that consists of all the old and wise men of his nation, which perhaps is two hundred people. Nothing of moment is undertaken, be it war, peace, selling of land or traffic, without advising with them, and, which is more, with the young men too. It is admirable to consider how powerful the kings are, and yet how they move by the breath of the people. I have had occasion to be in council with them upon treaties for land, and to adjust the terms of trade."

"They speak little, but fervently and with elegance. I have never seen more natural sagacity." . . . "And he will deserve the name of wise who outwits them in any treaty about a thing they understand. When the purchase was agreed, great promises passed between us of kindness and good-neighborhood, and that the English and Indians must live in love as long as the sun gave light, which done, another made a speech to the Indians in the name of the sachamakers or kings, first to tell them what was done, next to charge and command them to love the Christians, and particularly to live in peace with me and the people under my government, that many governors had been in the river, but that no governor had come himself to live and stay here before, and having now such an one, who had treated them well, they should never do him or his any wrong; at every sentence of which they shouted and said 'Amen' in their way."

CHAPTER IV.

THE BOUNDARY QUESTION—REVOLUTION IN ENGLAND.

1684-1689.

ONE of the subjects that caused the greatest solicitude in the mind of William Penn during his first sojourn in his colony, was a controversy with the proprietary of Maryland in relation to boundaries. To obtain an amicable adjustment of the matter in dispute, he had two interviews with Lord Baltimore, who treated him with courtesy and respect, but they could not agree, and there appeared to be no alternative but to refer the whole subject to the legal tribunals in England. In the meantime Lord Baltimore sent an agent to make a formal demand of all the country south of the fortieth degree of north latitude, both in the province of Pennsylvania and the territories annexed; and this not being acceded to, a party from Maryland under the command of Colonel George Talbott, in the spring of 1684, made forcible entry on several plantations in the lower counties. He came within five miles of New Castle, and there erected a fort of the bodies of trees, raised a breastwork and palisaded the same and placed armed men therein. The mayor of that town, together with the sheriff and magistrates, went to the fort and demanded of Colonel Talbott the reason of his proceedings, being a warlike invasion of the right of his majesty's subjects never in his possession. He answered them, after having bid them stand off (presenting guns at their breasts), that he had the Lord Baltimore's commission for what he did.

The governor and council at Philadelphia sent a copy of Penn's answer to Lord Baltimore's demand, showing the grounds of their refusal, and at the same time took legal measures to reinstate the persons who had been dispossessed, and if necessary to have the invaders prosecuted according to law.

"Lord Baltimore claimed by his charter the whole country as far as the fortieth degree. Penn replied, just as the Dutch and the agents of the Duke of York had always urged, that the charter of Maryland included only lands that were still unoccupied; that the banks of the Delaware had been purchased, appropriated and colonized before that charter was written. For more than fifty years the country had been in the hands of the Dutch and their successors, and during that whole period the claim of Lord Baltimore had always been resisted. The answer of Penn was true, and conformed to English law as applied to the colonies." *

The claim set up by Lord Baltimore, if successful, would have taken all the lands on the western side of the Delaware from the city of Philadelphia to the capes; it would have given Maryland the command of Delaware Bay; and would have deprived Penn of several valuable seaports. The peaceable course he pursued was in striking contrast with the warlike demonstration of Colonel Talbott.

About the time these events occurred, William Penn found it incumbent on him to return to England. He received advice that the members of his society in the mother country were suffering under severe persecution on account of their religion; their meetings were broken up by armed troops, and many hundreds of men and women, separated from their families, were confined in noisome prisons, where some had remained for years and others were released only by death. He had reason to believe that his personal

---

* "Bancroft's History of United States," II., 388. See "Janney's Life of Penn," for a full statement of the controversy.

influence and exertions might be instrumental to mitigate their sufferings.

The controversy respecting the boundaries of Pennsylvania and Maryland was soon to be brought before "the Lords of the Committee of Trade and Plantations." Lord Baltimore had already gone over to urge his claim; it was therefore highly important that Penn should be present to protect his own interests and those of the province. In addition to these considerations, we may reasonably conclude, that his desire to join his family, from which he had been separated nearly two years, was not least among the motives that determined him to return to England.

Having determined to embark in the Ketch Endeavor, he commissioned the provincial council to act in his stead, of which Thomas Lloyd was president, to whom he intrusted the keeping of the Great Seal. Nicholas Moore, Wm. Welch, Wm. Wood, Robt. Turner, and John Eckley were commissioned as provincial judges for two years; his cousin, Colonel Markham, was secretary, and James Harrison his steward, had charge of his house and manor at Pennsbury. His arrangements being completed, he embarked on the 12th of the sixth month (August), 1684, greatly to the regret of the whole country, for he had by his uniform justice and kindness endeared himself to all.

After a passage of about seven weeks he landed within seven miles of his own residence. Having enjoyed some days of rest and refreshment at home, he went to wait upon the king and duke, who received him very graciously. He found that the government was less favorably disposed towards religious liberty than it had been before he left the country—it was "sour and stern, and resolved to hold the reins of power with a stiffer hand than heretofore, especially over those who were observed to be church or state dissenters." He concluded, however, to take his old post as an advocate of liberty of conscience, and was an instrument of great good in pleading the cause of the oppressed.

The question relating to boundaries between the colonies of Lord Baltimore and William Penn was brought before the committee of trade and plantations, and after both parties had been fully heard, "it was decided that the tract of Delaware did not constitute a part of Maryland."

By an order of council dated 13th of November, 1685, it was decided that the lands intended to be granted by the Lord Baltimore's patent were only cultivated and inhabited by savages, and that the part then in dispute was inhabited and planted by Christians, at and before the date of the Lord Baltimore's patent, as it had been ever since to that time and continued as a distinct colony from that of Maryland." It was therefore ordered that "for avoiding further difference," the tract of land between the river and bay of Delaware, and Chesapeake Bay be divided into two equal parts.

The line designated by this order is the boundary between the States of Delaware and Maryland, but the line between Pennsylvania and Maryland, notwithstanding the many efforts made by Penn for its adjustment, continued in dispute during the remainder of his life, and was not finally settled until the year 1762, when it was run by "two ingenious mathematicians," Charles Mason and Jeremiah Dixon, who came from England for that purpose; hence it is called Mason and Dixon's line.

In the winter of 1684–5, King Charles II. died of apoplexy, and his brother, James, Duke of York, peaceably succeeded to the throne under the title of James II. James, while Duke of York, had for many years been the friend and patron of William Penn, whom he admitted to terms of familiar intercourse, not usual between a prince and a subject. This partiality on the part of the duke arose, in the first place, from his great regard for Admiral Penn; and was, doubtless, confirmed and augmented by the agreeable manners and excellent qualities of his son. After his accession

Peace Principles Exemplified. 89

to the throne he continued to manifest the same regard, which as it gave Penn ready access to the royal closet, enabled him to use his influence for the relief of many, both of his own and other religious persuasions, who were suffering for conscience sake.

Soon after the accession of James II. the friends petitioned for the release of upwards of 1400 of their members of both sexes imprisoned in England and Wales, only for worshipping God according to their sense of duty and for conscientiously refusing to swear. Their liberation did not take place for a year after their case was brought before the king, and there is reason to believe it was then done chiefly through the personal influence and intercession of William Penn. Some of these patient sufferers for the cause of truth had been twelve or fifteen years and upwards in prison.

While Penn was engaged in obtaining an adjustment of boundaries and pleading the cause of religious liberty in England, his friends in Pennsylvania were pushing forward their improvements in building and planting, and performing their novitiate in legislation. The increase of population continued to be rapid, the colony was peaceful and prosperous; but among those concerned in the government there were some jealousies and dissensions, which being reported to the proprietary, with much exaggeration, called forth his paternal admonition.

The provincial council was too large a body to perform with efficiency the executive functions intrusted to them; they neglected to comply with the instructions of the proprietary, and he came to the conclusion to change the form of the executive. He accordingly appointed in the 12th month, 1686, five commissioners, any three of whom were authorized to act on his behalf. Their names were Thomas Lloyd, Nicholas Moore, James Claypole, Robert Turner and John Eckley. Their appointment seems to have been attended with a happy effect; their administration was prudent, steady and efficient. Nothing further of note occurs in the history of the province in the succeeding two years, during which the colonists enjoyed the blessings of domestic tranquillity.

In the meantime Penn was frequently in attendance on the king advising him to measures of clemency, moderation and justice, which would have established his throne, but the infatuated monarch took counsel from bigoted priests and venal courtiers, and was led to pursue an arbitrary and oppressive course which alienated the affections of his people. In addition to other unpopular measures, his open profession of the Roman Catholic religion and the favor he showed the priests produced great dissatisfaction among his Protestant subjects.

The king's son-in-law, William, Prince of Orange, being a Protestant, and having the confidence of the English people, was invited by many of the nobility and gentry to come and assume the reins of government. He came, and was joined by persons of the highest rank—part of the king's army deserted to his standard—and the popular feeling was so strongly manifested in his favor that the king, in the year 1688, abdicated his throne and retired to France.

The convention having declared the throne vacant, the Prince and Princess of Orange were crowned in 1689, as joint sovereigns, under the title of William and Mary.

Soon after the revolution in England, the situation of William Penn became critical in the extreme; the influence he had possessed in the late reign was now turned against him; he was regarded by many as being disaffected to the government, a Jesuit in disguise, and an enemy to the Protestant cause. To withdraw to Pennsylvania, where he knew his presence was needed, would subject him to the imputation of having fled to escape punishment, and thus give color to the aspersions of his enemies. To remain was hazardous, but honorable, and therefore he determined to stay and pursue his usual avocations.

While walking in Whitehall, he was sent for by the lords of the council then sitting. In reply to their questions he assured them, "he had done nothing but what he could answer before God and all the princes in the world; that he loved his country and the Protestant religion above his life, and never acted against either; that all he ever aimed at in his public endeavors was no other than what the prince himself had declared for; that King James was always his friend, and his father's friend, and in gratitude he was the king's, and did, ever as much as in him lay, influence him to his true interest."

Although nothing appeared against him, he was required to give sureties for his appearance the first day of the next term. At the next term his case was continued to the Easter term following, when nothing being laid to his charge he was cleared in open court.

In the year 1689, the Act of Toleration was passed by Parliament and approved by the king. This act provided that none of the penal laws should be construed to extend to those dissenters who should take the oaths to the present government, and a clause was inserted for the relief of the Society of Friends, accepting from them, instead of the oaths, a solemn promise to be faithful to the king and queen. So great had been the progress of public sentiment, that a bill abolishing the tests, by which dissenters were excluded from parliament, was, in conformity with the king's wishes, passed by the House of Commons, but it was rejected by the peers. There can be no doubt that the sufferings of the Friends and other dissenters were instrumental in preparing the minds of the people for this salutary change in the policy of the government; but to Penn more than to any other man must it be attributed. His numerous publications in its favor had been silently operating, while the liberal policy of his own government, and the remarkable prosperity of his province, must have exerted a considerable influence on the public mind.

In Pennsylvania, Thomas Lloyd, a minister of the Society of Friends and a man of excellent character and abilities, had for some years been performing the executive functions of the government, first as president of the council and afterwards as chairman of the commissioners; but becoming weary of public affairs he requested to be released from the burden, to which William Penn, by a letter written in 1687, reluctantly consented. As no other Friend, properly qualified, was found willing to accept the office of deputy governor, William Penn appointed to that station Captain John Blackwell, who had formerly held an important trust under the British government, and was highly recommended for his virtue and fidelity. In Penn's letter of instructions, dated 1688, he directs Governor Blackwell to send him a copy of the laws, which he had often requested before, but in vain; to be careful that speedy and impartial justice be done, to see that the widow, the orphan and the absent be particularly regarded in their rights; to have a special care that the sheriffs and clerks of the peace impose not upon the people, and finally, " to rule the meek meekly, and those that will not be ruled, rule with authority."

Governor Blackwell met the assembly in the third month 1689, but by reason of some misunderstanding or dissension between him and some of the council, the public affairs were not transacted in harmony, and but little business was done during his administration, which lasted only until the twelfth month, when, by the advice of Penn, he resigned and returned to England. One cause of disagreement was, the governor's attempt to raise a militia, which being a warlike measure inconsistent with the principles of the colonists, was resisted by them.

Peace Principles Exemplified. 95

The people of Pennsylvania and the neighboring Indian tribes had lived on terms of the most cordial friendship, and each had performed many kind offices for the other; but in the year 1688, the inhabitants of Philadelphia and places adjacent were alarmed with the report of an intended insurrection of the Indians to cut off all the English on a certain appointed day. This was communicated by an Indian woman of West New Jersey, to an old Dutch inhabitant near Chester, and was soon after corroborated by another rumor that three families about nine miles from that place had actually been destroyed. It was also said that five hundred Indians were collected in pursuance of their design to kill the English.

When these alarming reports reached Philadelphia the council was in session, and Caleb Pusey, one of its members, a Friend in high standing, from Chester county, offered to go to the place where the Indians were said to be assembled, provided the council would appoint five others to go with him *unarmed*. This being agreed to, they immediately proceeded thither on horseback, but instead of meeting five hundred warriors, as was reported, they found the old king quietly lying on his bed, the women at work in the fields and the children at play. When they entered the wigwam, the king asked them very mildly what they all came for? They told him the report which the Indian woman had raised, and asked whether the Indians had anything against the English? He appeared much displeased at the report and said: "The woman ought to be burnt to death; and that they had nothing against the English;" adding: "'Tis true there are about fifteen pounds yet behind of our pay for the land that William Penn bought, but as you are still on it and improving it to your own use, we are not in haste for our pay; but when the English come to settle it, we expect to be paid." This the messengers assured him should be done. One of the company further expressed himself to this effect: "That as the great God, who made the world and all things therein, consequently made all mankind, both Indians and English, so his love was extended to all; which was plainly shown by his causing the rain and dew to fall on the ground of both Indians and English alike, that it might equally produce what each of them planted on it, for the sustenance of life. And also, by his making the sun to shine equally on all, both Indians and English, he manifested his love to all, so they were mutually bound to love one another." The king answered, "What you say is very true, and as God has given you corn, I would advise you to get it in (it

PEACE PRINCIPLES EXEMPLIFIED. 97

being then harvest time); for we intend you no harm."

The return of the messengers dispelled the fears of the people, and the result evinced the wisdom of the policy uniformly pursued by the friends of William Penn.

CHAPTER V.

TROUBLES IN EUROPE AND AMERICA.

1689-95.

WHILE the colonists of Pennsylvania were peacefully pursuing their industrial occupations, enjoying the blessings of civil and religious liberty, and founding in the wilderness an asylum for the oppressed of every land, the nations of Europe professing the Christian name were involved in a fierce conflict of arms, spreading desolation and distress over populous countries. Wars were waged on account of religion in which all the principles of Christianity were set at naught, and wars to maintain the balance of power in Europe wasted the blood and treasure of the English people, without any adequate returns.

William Penn writing to his friends in Pennsylvania, in the Tenth month, 1689, after exhorting them to the exercise of Christian charity, thus continues: "For matters here; as to myself I am well and free; and for the church of God liberty continues. But in the nations of Europe, great wars and rumors of wars, such as have not been almost from the beginning, suns are turning into darkness and moons into blood; for the notable day is at the door.".... "Sanctify therefore the Lord in your hearts; be satisfied in him, and in your lot, and walk worthy of his daily mercy, and care over you."

In the year 1690, Penn was again brought before the lords of the council upon an accusation of holding a correspondence with the late King James; and they requiring sureties for his appearance, he appealed to King William himself, who after a conference of nearly two hours, inclined to acquit him; but to please some of the council, he was held upon bail, for a while, and in Trinity-term the same year was again discharged.

He was attacked a third time, and his name inserted in a proclamation wherein he, with eighteen other persons, were charged with adhering to the king's enemies, but no proofs of the charge being found, he was again cleared by order of the court of the Kings-bench, at Michaelmas-term, 1690.

Being now at liberty he proposed to go a second time to Pennsylvania, and published proposals, for a second settlement there, which probably was designed to be on the Susquehanna. His plans were again frustated by a fresh accusation against him founded on the oath of William

Fuller, who was afterwards declared by Parliament "a cheat and a notorious impostor." A warrant being issued for Penn's apprehension, he narrowly escaped being arrested at his return from the funeral of George Fox, who was buried in London on the 16th of the Eleventh month of 1690–91. In writing to the widow, on the 13th, who was in Lancashire, he said: "I am to be the teller to thee of sorrowful tidings, in some respect which is this: that thy dear husband and my beloved and dear friend, finished his glorious testimony this night, about half an hour after nine, being sensible to the last breath. Oh! he is gone, and has left us in the storm that is over our heads, surely in great mercy to him, but as an evidence to us of sorrow to come."

On being informed of this fresh accusation, Penn thought it most prudent to postpone his departure, for should he leave England while he was under suspicion and subject to arrest, his removal would be construed by his enemies as an evidence of his guilt. He therefore took private lodgings in London and lived in seclusion. Here he devoted himself to study, to writing and religious meditations; being also frequently visited by his friends, among whom were John Locke and others eminent for their worth.

While the proprietary of Pennsylvania was compelled by false accusations to forego his cherished purpose of returning thither, as his permanent home, the affairs of his colony were suffering for want of his paternal care. The three lower counties, called the territories, now constituting the State of Delaware, had at the request of their inhabitants been united with the province under one government, allowing to every county an equal number of representatives. During the absence of Penn some jealousies had crept in between them; the province was large, its population was rapidly increasing, and it must have been manifest to all that the balance of power would soon preponderate in its favor. For this reason some of the inhabitants of the territories began to think they had distinct and even conflicting interests, which led to a misunderstanding.

On Governor Blackwell's resignation, the executive duties devolved on the council, and Thomas Lloyd, not being willing to refuse his assistance in this emergency, acted again as president. In order to compose all differences, Penn proposed three forms of executive power, and left to the decision of the council which should be adopted—either the council, five commissioners, or a deputy-governor. The majority favored a deputy-governor, and were satisfied with Thomas Lloyd, but the councilmen from the territories preferred the five commissioners, and finding themselves outnumbered, withdrew from the council, and returned home. Thomas Lloyd sent a deputation to New Castle to confer with them, but his efforts to reconcile them were unavailing.

The proprietary, with much reluctance, submitted to the separation, and commissioned Thomas Lloyd as governor of the province. William Markham, who appears to have gone with the seceders, was placed over the territories as their executive.

Although Penn had consented with great reluctance to this arrangement, it answered beyond his expectations in restoring harmony; and as both parties were sensible that he had been grieved at their dissensions, they endeavored to relieve his mind by a joint letter from the two deputy-governors and the members of council, expressive of their affection and of their earnest desire for his return to the province.

About the time these political changes were effected, dissensions of a far more painful tendency arose in relation to the doctrines and discipline of the Society of Friends. The dispute originated with George Keith, a prominent minister and an author of several religious works. He was a Scotchman, had lived much in England, had travelled with Penn on the continent, and was employed for one year as the principal teacher in the public school at Philadelphia.

He had been much respected, but now appeared ambitious of greater distinction as a leader in the society, proposing and urging new regulations in its discipline, complaining that there was "too great a slackness therein," and accusing some of the most valued ministers of preaching false doctrines, although it was thought they preached the same views he had formerly advocated in his writings. Another objection urged by him against some of the most influential members was the part they took in the government of the province, alleging that, by acting as magistrates and executing the penal laws against malefactors, they violated their principles. The last of these charges had reference principally to the course pursued in arresting a privateer, named Babbitt, who took a sloop from the wharf at Philadelphia, proceeded down the river and committed several robberies. A warrant being issued for his apprehension, Peter Boss and some others pursued him in a boat and took him and his crew without any warlike weapon.

At length Keith having set up a separate meeting in Philadelphia, and being in the practice of defaming the characters of Friends, the meeting of ministers disowned him, which act was confirmed by the yearly meetings of Burlington and London. He and Thomas Budd were presented by the grand-jury of Philadelphia for defaming Samuel Jennings, a provincial judge, and being found guilty, were fined five pounds each. These fines, however, were never exacted. The meetings set up by Keith and his adherents threatened to make a formidable schism in the society, but he having gone to England, was ordained by the Bishop of London, and returned to Pennsylvania a clergyman in orders. This conduct so disgusted his followers, that many of them returned to the society, and the schism was finally healed.

The political and religious dissensions which for a while disturbed the tranquillity of colonial life in Pennsylvania, being communicated to William Penn, increased the burden of his cares and occasioned much solicitude, which he expressed in affectionate letters to his friends in the colony.

In the autumn of 1692, a commission was granted by the sovereigns, William and Mary, to Benjamin Fletcher, Governor of New York, directing him to take under his jurisdiction the province of Pennsylvania, and the territories annexed. This step was urged by the enemies of the proprietary as necessary for the safety of the colony. It was said that the French and Indians threatened the frontier settlements, that no defence had been provided by the colonial government, and that the province and the territories being at variance, no efficient administration of the laws could be expected. They did not fail to adduce the religious dissensions among the Friends as another reason why they were unfit to govern, and the prosecution against George Keith, for defamation, being misrepresented by his party, was triumphantly held up as an evidence that the Quakers as well as others could persecute for religion.

William Penn was sorely tried—his troubles seemed to increase and press upon him with accumulated weight. Cast down from a high and honored station in society, accused of being an enemy to the government and to the Protestant cause, impoverished by expenditures for his province, and now that province, the object of his hopes, withdrawn from under his government, there was needed but one drop more to fill the measure of his afflictions. That drop too was added. His wife, one of the loveliest and best of women, was visibly sinking in health, and her decline was attributed to intense anxiety, induced by her husband's calamities.

But although perplexed with care, and burdened with grief, he was not forsaken; having the solace of an approving conscience, and an abiding trust in the providence of God, who often permits his servants to be tried in the furnace of affliction, in order to perfect their refinement; who removes from them the attractions of the world, in order to draw them nearer to himself, and when they have relinquished all other dependence, manifests that the arm of his power is sufficient to uphold them, and to cause "all things to work together for their good."

In the latter part of the year 1693, through the intercession of some noblemen, who had long been his friends, the case of William Penn was again brought before King William, who, being satisfied of his innocence, signified his wish that he should consider himself entirely at liberty.

His wife, who had tenderly sympathized with him in all his trials, was permitted to see him again restored to liberty; but in the following month she was removed by death, and he was again plunged into a depth of affliction, which could be alleviated only by the consolations of religion and the lenient hand of time.

During Penn's seclusion from the world, which continued nearly three years, his vigorous and active mind was not unemployed. He wrote a number of religious works, one of which is entitled, "Some Fruits of Solitude in Reflections, and Maxims relating to the Conduct of Human Life." This work embraces a compendium of practical wisdom that has seldom been equalled in the same compass, being the result of much experience in the affairs of life, and deep reflection on its cares and vicissitudes.

In the preface he alludes, in the spirit of a true Christian, to his seclusion from the world:

"READER:—This enchiridion I present thee with is the fruit of solitude, a school few care to learn in, though none instructs us better. Some parts of it are the results of serious reflection, others the flashing of lucid intervals, written for private satisfaction, and now published for an help to human conduct. The author blesseth God for his retirement, and kisses that gentle hand which led him into it; for though it should prove barren to the world, it can never do so to him. He has now had some time he could call his own—a property he was never so much master of before—in which he has taken a view of himself and the world, and observed wherein he has hit or missed the mark; what might have been done; what mended and what avoided in human conduct; together with the omissions and excesses of others, as well societies and governments as private families and persons."

William Penn produced at this time another work of great value and importance, entitled,

"An Essay towards the Present and Future Peace of Europe, by the Establishment of an European Diet, Parliament, or Estates." It was written in the year 1695. In the first section he refers to the bloody wars then being waged in "Hungary, Germany, Flanders, Ireland, and at sea: the mortality of sickly and languishing camps and navies, and the mighty prey the devouring winds and waves have made upon ships and men since the year 1688." He draws a contrast between the misery entailed by war, and the blessings conferred by peace, and then proceeds to show "the means of peace, which is justice rather than war." "Government is an expedient against confusion." It is instituted for the prevention or cure of disorder and the punishment of crime, in order that men may not be judges of their own cause or avengers of their own wrongs. As in civil society, individuals and corporations submit their differences to the decision of courts established and governed by law; so should the nations of Europe establish a tribunal and enact laws for the settlement of international disputes. The fourth section, containing the gist of the essay, is here subjoined:

"Of a general peace, or the peace of Europe and the means of it.

"In my first section I showed the desirable-

PEACE PRINCIPLES EXEMPLIFIED. 109

ness of peace; in my next the truest means of it, viz., justice, and not war. And in my last, that this justice was the fruit of government, as government itself was the result of society, which first came from a reasonable design of men of peace. Now if the sovereign *princes* of Europe who represent that society, or independent state of men that was previous to the obligations of society, would, for the same reason that engaged men first in society, viz., *Love of Peace and Order*, agree to meet by their stated deputies in a General Diet, Estates, or Parliament, and there establish rules of justice for sovereign princes to observe one to another; and thus to meet yearly, or once in two or three years at farthest, or as they shall see cause, and to be styled, The Sovereign or Imperial Diet, Parliament, or State of Europe; before which sovereign assembly should be brought all differences depending between one sovereign and another that cannot be made up by private embassies before the session begins, and that if any of the sovereignties that constitute these imperial states shall refuse to submit their claim or pretension to them, or to abide and perform the judgment thereof and seek their remedy by arms, or delay their compliance beyond the time prefixed in their resolutions, all the other sovereignties, united as one strength, shall compel the submission and performance of the sentence, with damages to the suffering party, and charges to the sovereignties that obliged their submission. To be sure, Europe would quietly obtain the so much desired and needed peace to her harassed inhabitants; no sovereignty in Europe having the power, and, therefore, cannot show the will, to dispute the conclusion, and consequently peace would be procured and continued in Europe."

The proposal embraced in this essay excited much interest at the time of its publication, and has since been frequently referred to by the advocates of universal peace. It contains suggestions leading to a peace policy which has recently been more fully developed by enlightened thinkers in Europe and America, as expressed in the conventions of the friends of peace at Paris, Brussels, Frankfort, and The Hague.

Since the time of Penn, some progress has been made: the principles of international law are better understood, the power of public opinion in controlling legislation has greatly increased, and constitutional governments are more numerous.

The only objectionable feature in the plan proposed by Penn is the coercive power to be exercised in *compelling* the refractory sovereigns to abide by the decisions of the General Diet. If the compulsion should be exercised by force of arms—bombarding their cities, devastating their country, and killing their people—it would be such a departure from the principles of peace and good-will to men, as would frustrate the whole design. But if the compulsory measures should be, to put the refractory government under the ban of public opinion throughout the world, to declare non-intercourse until a reconciliation could be effected, or to withhold the advantages of commercial reciprocity, there could be no reasonable objection to such compulsory measures, and they would probably be sufficient.

Public opinion has been called the queen of the world; its power in controlling legislation is great and increasing. In order that it may exercise a salutary influence, it must be enlightened by general education and the inculcation of Christian principles. The admiration of military glory must be discountenanced, the spirit of retaliation must be supplanted by the Christ-like spirit of forgiveness, and the narrow sentiment of patriotism should be merged in the nobler sentiment of universal brotherhood.

The Christian church is responsible for the continuance of the barbarous custom of war, which is utterly repugnant to the precepts and example of the Messiah. This sentiment is forcibly expressed in the following passage from

Sumner's eloquent "Oration on the True Grandeur of Nations:"

"It cannot be doubted that this strange and unblessed conjunction of the Christian clergy with war has had no little influence in blinding the world to the truth now beginning to be recognized, that *Christianity forbids the whole custom of war*.

"Individual interests are mingled with prevailing errors, and are so far concerned in maintaining them, that it is not surprising how reluctantly military men yield to this truth. They are naturally like lawyers, as described by Voltaire, 'the conservators of ancient barbarous usages,' but that these usages—especially that the impious Trial by Battle—should obtain countenance in the Christian church, is one of those anomalies which make us feel the weakness of our nature and the elevation of Christian truth. It is important to observe as the testimony of history that for some time after the Apostles, while the lamp of Christianity burnt pure and bright, not only the Fathers of the church held it unlawful for Christians to bear arms; but those who came within its pale abstained from their use, although at the cost of life, *thus renouncing not only the umpirage of war*, but even the right of self-defence. Marcellus, the Centurion, threw

Peace Principles Exemplified. 113

down his military belt at the head of the legion, and in the face of the standards declared, with a loud voice, that he *would no longer serve in the army,* for *he had become a Christian;* others followed his example. It was not until Christianity became corrupted, that its followers became soldiers, and its priests learned to minister at the altar of the God of Battles."

CHAPTER VI.

COLONIAL AFFAIRS AND PENN'S SECOND MARRIAGE.

1693-1701.

COLONEL BENJAMIN FLETCHER, governor of New York, was commissioned by the king and queen as governor of Pennsylvania, in the autumn of 1692, but did not receive the commission until some months later. In the spring of 1693, he notified Governor Lloyd, of Pennsylvania, that he intended to assume the reins of government, and accordingly he came to Philadelphia, for that purpose, attended by a military retinue. Notwithstanding the separation of the territories from the province, he summoned the representatives of both to meet him in Philadelphia. In this writ the charter and laws of Pennsylvania were disregarded, the number of delegates being diminished, and the time and form of the election changed.

The first business proposed to the assembly, by

the governor, was a requisition from the queen for aid, in men and money, to defend the frontiers of New York against the incursions of the French and Indians. The war then existing between France and England, growing out of the accession of William and Mary to the throne, had extended its ravages to their colonies in North America, and the French commanders in Canada had resorted to the barbarous expedient of subsidizing the Indians and inciting them to murder their English neighbors. A predatory warfare ensued, in which the colonies of New England and New York were chiefly engaged in repelling the savages, who surprised and destroyed Schenectady and some other frontier settlements. The alliance of the Mengwe, or Five Nations (Iroquois), was sought by both parties, and finally secured by the English at great expense, to defray which, in part, was the object of the subsidy now demanded.

The assembly resolutely asserted its privileges, but finally passed a bill imposing a tax of a penny a pound on the clear value of real and personal estate and a poll-tax of six shillings a head, which they presented to the king and queen with a request that "one-half thereof might be allowed to the governor." Fletcher at first refused the bill because nothing was granted for the defence of New York, and he even threatened to annex Pennsylvania to that province; but finally he approved this as well as other bills that were presented to him, and confirmed the laws before existing in the colony. He then dissolved the assembly by their own advice, and, having appointed William Markham lieutenant-governor, departed for New York.

The following year, 1694, Governor Fletcher made another requisition for aid to New York; but, having found by experience that it was in vain to expect military supplies from men who were conscientiously opposed to war, he requested of them means to clothe and feed the Indians in order to secure their continued friendship to the provinces. The assembly laid a tax similar to that imposed the previous year, which amounted to seven hundred and sixty pounds; but they stipulated for the payment of two hundred pounds each to Thomas Lloyd and William Markham for their services while acting as deputies of the proprietary, and the remainder to be appropriated to the general expenses of the government. "Fletcher rejected the bill, and the assembly, asserting their right to appropriate their money at their pleasure, was dissolved."

Soon after this, the government was restored to William Penn, by a patent from the king and queen, dated August, 1694. His application to be reinstated had been warmly seconded by some of his friends among the nobility, who represented to the king and council that the disorders charged upon the province had been greatly exaggerated by report, and even so far as true, had been occasioned by the proprietary's absence. He was now earnestly desirous of removing to the province; but the situation of his domestic affairs, and probably the state of his finances, obliged him to defer it.

In the autumn of 1694, he appointed Captain William Markham, his lieutenant-governor; Thomas Lloyd, his former governor, having died a few months previously. In the death of Thomas Lloyd the colony lost one of its most beloved and honored citizens. He was one of the few who, being qualified by abilities and virtue for the highest stations in society, yet through modesty or humility decline them, until urged by the public voice and called by a sense of duty to accept the post of trust and honor. He was the only one among the many deputies, employed by Penn, whose administration gave satisfaction to both the proprietary and the people.

Governor Markham, disregarding the laws of Pennsylvania, pursued Fletcher's plan of calling the assembly, and having, without their consent, dissolved both the council and assembly, they, at their next meeting in 1696, made a spirited remonstrance against his encroachments, and succeeded in obtaining his consent to a "bill of settlement," whereby the power of the assembly was increased, being authorized to originate bills, to adjourn and reassemble at pleasure, and to be indissoluble during the time for which they were elected. In return for these concessions they passed a bill to raise three hundred pounds for the support of government and the relief of the distressed Indians in New York.

The appointment of Markham, as governor, was in accordance with a promise Penn had made to the committee of trade and plantations, that he would "appoint the same person to be his deputy-governor" who was then serving under Colonel Fletcher, and to satisfy the colonists he appointed two Friends, John Goodson and Samuel Carpenter, assistants of Markham, in the administration.

From the time William Penn was reinstated in his government, until his arrival in the province in 1699, a period of five years, there are no incidents of importance on record concerning the colony. During this period, the paucity of materials for history may be considered an evidence of domestic tranquillity, and there is reason to believe that the colonists of Pennsylvania then enjoyed a degree of prosperity and happiness that seldom falls to the lot of humanity.

In the spring of 1696, William Penn was married to his second wife, who was Hannah, the daughter of Thomas Callowhill, and granddaughter of Dennis Hollister, both eminent merchants of Bristol and members of the Society of Friends. She proved to be a true help-meet for him, being a woman of superior understanding and great prudence.

About five weeks after this event, he experienced another vicissitude from joy to grief, in the death of his eldest son, Springett Penn, who died of consumption in the 21st year of his age. He was a young man of great promise, concerning whom his father has left a touching memorial.

After Penn's restoration to his proprietary rights, there was, in the public mind, a reaction in his favor, and he rose higher than ever in the estimation of his friends. He travelled as a minister in England and Ireland, his meetings being attended by large crowds to whom he preached with acceptance the Gospel of Christ.

In the summer of 1699, he prepared to fulfil his long-cherished purpose of removing with his wife and daughter to Pennsylvania for a permanent residence. On the 9th of the 7th month (September, O. S.), 1699, he sailed in the ship "Canterbury" from Cowes, in the Isle of Wight, having two days previously addressed, from on board the ship, an epistle to the members of his own religious society, which concludes as follows:

"I must leave you, but I never can forget you; for my love to you has been even as David's and Jonathan's, above the love of women: and suffer me to say that, to my power, I have from the first endeavored to serve you (and my poor country), and that, at my own charges, with an upright mind, however *misunderstood and treated* by some, whom I heartily forgive. Accept you my services; and ever love and remember, my dear friends and brethren, your old, true, and affectionate friend, brother, and servant in Christ Jesus,

"WILLIAM PENN."

Previous to his embarkation, the Friends in England gave him three certificates addressed to the meetings of Friends in Pennsylvania, which may be seen in the first Book of Records of Philadelphia monthly meeting. These documents show that he was in full unity with the meetings of his own society, and greatly beloved among them. The first certificate is from the "Meeting of Ministering Friends" in London; which, after alluding to his eminent services in the gospel ministry, his successful efforts in pleading the cause of the oppressed, his tribulations, arising from the malice of his enemies, and his meekness in forgiving them, concludes by stating that he parted with their meeting in great love, and was in true unity as an approved minister of Christ. The second is from the "Men's Meeting of Friends, in the city of Bristol," and the third, from the monthly meeting at Horsham, England, both of which express in strong terms their unity with him in the bonds of Christian love.

After a tedious voyage of more than three months, the ship arrived at Chester, on the 1st day of the Tenth month (December, O. S.), 1699. Having exchanged salutations with his friends in Chester, Penn proceeded in the ship to Philadelphia, where he was greeted by the inhabitants with joy and respect. The city had lately been visited by the yellow fever, which carried off many of the inhabitants, and spread a general gloom over the community.

Before the landing of Penn and his family the fever had ceased, and nothing could have been better adapted to dispel the gloom that remained than the long-desired arrival of their beloved and venerated governor.

Among the passengers who came over with Penn, in the ship "Canterbury," was James Logan, whom he had engaged to accompany him to Pennsylvania as his secretary. Logan was a man of great abilities and learning. He acted a conspicuous and useful part in the affairs of the colony, as secretary of the province, commissioner of property, for some time president of the council, and afterwards chief-justice of Pennsylvania.

The governor and his family, with his secretary, went, on their arrival, to lodge at Edward Shippen's, where they remained about a month. Penn then took a house, known as the slate-roof house, on Second street, between Chestnut and Walnut, at the southeast corner of Norris's alley. Here was born, about two months after their arrival, his son John, the only one of his children born in this country, and therefore called "the American."

Soon after his arrival Penn met the assembly, when the chief business transacted was the passage of two laws for the suppression of piracy and illicit trade.

In the First month of the year 1700 he attended the monthly meeting of Friends in Philadelphia, and laid before them his concern for the welfare of the negroes and Indians, which, he said, had long engaged the attention of his mind. He exhorted the members to the full discharge of their duty towards these people; but more especially in regard to their spiritual improvement; that they might have the advantage of attending religious meetings, and the benefit of being duly instructed in the Christian religion. Hence a meeting was appointed more especially for the negroes once a month, and means were used to have more frequent meetings with the Indians, Penn taking part of the charge upon himself, particularly the manner of holding it, and the procuring of interpreters.

It appears on the colonial records that Governor Penn, in the spring of 1700, brought before the provincial council a law for regulating the marriages of negroes, which was approved by that body, but lost in the popular branch. It is stated that "he mourned over the state of the slaves, but his attempts to improve their condition by legal enactments were defeated in the house of assembly." The rise and progress of the testimony against slavery in the Society of Friends is a subject of much interest, evincing in its gradual development and ultimate triumph the certainty and safety of Divine guidance. George Fox was one of the earliest to call the attention of his brethren to this subject. While in Barbadoes, in the year 1671, he advised those who held slaves "to train them up in the fear of God," to cause their overseers to deal mildly and gently with them, and after certain years of servitude to set them free. In the year 1688 the subject of slavery was brought before the yearly meeting of Pennsylvania and

New Jersey, by some German Friends residing at Germantown, among whom Francis Daniel Pastorius was the most prominent. It was at that time not thought proper for the meeting to give a positive judgment, but the subject was revived frequently in after years, and the more it was examined the greater appeared to be the evil of slaveholding, until, after nearly a century of patient labor, it was made a disownable offence by the Philadelphia Yearly Meeting, in the year 1776. The same year that the American Congress proclaimed the equal and inalienable rights of man in the Declaration of Independence, the Society of Friends in Pennsylvania and New Jersey gave freedom to their slaves, and even provided some remuneration for their unrequited toil. It is an interesting fact that many of the Friends who manumitted their slaves were not satisfied to send them forth empty-handed from the house of bondage, but made them such reparation as justice . required. In some meetings committees were appointed to ascertain the amount that was equitably due from the master to the slave.

William Penn at one time owned a few slaves, whom he liberated, as appears by a will he made in 1701, which is still extant, and contains this clause: "I give to my blacks their freedom, *as is under my hand already,* and to old Sam 100 acres, to be his children's, after he and his wife are dead, forever."*

In the spring or summer of 1700 Governor Penn, with his family, removed to Pennsbury Manor, his favorite place of residence. This beautiful estate was situated in Bucks county, four miles above Bristol, on the river Delaware. It comprised six thousand acres of fertile alluvial soil, mostly covered with majestic forests, there being at that time only ten acres under cultivation. The mansion was commodious and well furnished; it had on the first floor a large hall, used on public occasions for the meeting of the council, and the entertainment of strangers and the Indians.

Tradition relates that on one occasion, when he made a feast for his red brethren, a long table was spread for them in the avenue leading to the house, which was shaded by poplars, and among the viands provided were one hundred turkeys, besides venison and other meats.

In the spring of 1701 a treaty was made by Governor Penn, and some members of his council, with the Susquehanna Indians, for the preservation of peace, and the confirmation of titles to land conveyed in former treaties. It appears that Penn, before he returned to England in 1684, had taken measures to purchase the lands on the

---

* See "Janney's Life of Penn," chap. xxxi.

Susquehanna from the Five Nations (Iroquois), who claimed the right to them by conquest. These Indians resided principally in New York, and the purchase was effected through Thomas Dungan, governor of New York, who conveyed the same to Penn by deed, dated January 13, 1696, in consideration of £100 sterling. The Susquehanna Indians did not recognize the right of the Five Nations to make this sale, and in order to satisfy their demands, Penn entered into a treaty with two of their chiefs, whose deed, dated September 13, 1700, conveys the same lands, and confirms the sale made to Governor Dungan. But it appears there was still another chief claiming an interest in those lands, viz., Connoodaghoh, king of the Conostoga or Minquay Indians. To satisfy this claim Governor Penn and his council entered into a treaty of amity in Philadelphia, by which the sale of the lands on the Susquehanna was for the third time confirmed.

The conciliatory course pursued in dealing with these several tribes of Indians was eminently wise, for even in an economical point of view the peace policy of the Friends was more advantageous than the war policy often pursued in the other colonies.

For the prevention of abuses that were too frequently put upon the Indians, it was resolved in council that no person should be allowed to trade with them but such as Penn and his successors should approve and furnish with a license under his hand and seal. And, moreover, it was resolved that a company be formed to take proper measures to inspire the Indians with a true esteem of the Christian religion by setting before them good examples of probity and candor, both in commerce and behavior; and that "care should be taken to have them duly instructed in the fundamentals of Christianity."

At this time the people of the province and territories were under apprehensions of depredations being committed by pirates, who were said to be numerous on the coast; and in order to guard against them a watchman was stationed at Cape Henlopen, in the county of Sussex, who was to give notice to the sheriff of the county when any suspected vessel entered the capes, and the sheriffs of the several counties were to send the information by express till it should reach the governor at Philadelphia.

In the Sixth month, 1701, the governor convened the assembly in order to lay before them a letter from the king, requiring a contribution of £350 sterling, toward erecting forts on the frontiers of New York. He made them a short speech expressive of his regret that he was obliged to call them together sooner than he intended.

"But," he says, "the king's commands, by his letter to me now, have brought you hither at this time, which I now lay before you, and recommend to your serious consideration, since without it, it will be impossible to answer them." This requisition being for a warlike purpose, was extremely repugnant to the feelings both of the governor and assembly. He felt compelled by his fealty to the king to lay the letter before them, but in abstaining from expressing his own views he endeavored to cast the responsibility on the representatives of the people. They were thrown into a state of painful embarrassment; for if they refused the subsidy, they had reason to dread the displeasure of the British government; but most of the members being opposed to war, and representing a constituency who were chiefly Friends, they could not comply without a violation of their religious principles. After some days spent in deliberation they sent their answer in writing, declining to comply with the king's requisition, assigning as a reason, the taxes already levied, and the quit-rents due. They stated, moreover, that the adjacent colonies had done nothing in the matter, and therefore they postponed it to another session, desiring that the proprietary would represent their condition to the king, and assure him of their readiness to comply with his commands, "as far as their religious persuasions would permit." The members for the territories made a separate answer, alleging that the lower counties, though most exposed, were in a defenceless condition, being without arms or ammunition, and having neither militia, nor officers appointed to command them. They prayed, therefore, to be excused from "contributing to forts abroad while they were unable to build any for their own defence at home." This answer shows that the members from the territories were less imbued with the principles of Friends in relation to war than those of the province, and doubtless this was one cause of their frequent disagreements, for the pacific policy of Penn could only be carried into practice by persons thoroughly convinced of its feasibility.

The governor, having received the assembly's answer to the king's letter, dismissed it; but little more than two weeks elapsed before he received information from England which made it necessary to issue writs for the immediate election of another. He learned from the letters of his friends, that "strenuous endeavors were used by several united interests to procure an act of Parliament for annexing to the crown the several proprietary governments, for which purpose a bill was then before the House of Lords, which had been twice read, and though not likely to pass that session, there was no hope of staving it off longer than the next, unless the proprietary would make his appearance in person, and answer the charges brought against his government by evil-minded persons." His friends in England urged the necessity of his coming with as little delay as possible; the welfare of the province, as well as his own interest, seemed to require it, and he reluctantly consented to leave his adopted country to appear once more at his old post near the British court.

A new assembly having been elected, met in Philadelphia the 15th of the Seventh month, 1701, when the governor addressed them in a speech, expressing his regret that he was obliged to call them together so frequently, and stating the business which then required their attention on the eve of his departure for England. After expressing his reluctance to leave the country where he had promised himself a quiet home, and his intention to return and settle his family there, he thus continued: "Think, therefore, since all men are mortal, of some suitable expedient and provision for your safety, as well in your privileges as property, and you will find me ready to comply with whatever may render us happy by a nearer union of our interest. Review again your laws, propose new ones that may better your circumstances; and what you do, do it quickly, remembering that the Parliament sits the end of next month, and that the sooner I am there the safer."

While the assembly was in session, and the governor busily engaged in preparations for his departure, he was visited in Philadelphia by the sachems of the Susquehanna and Shawnese Indians, who, with some of their people, had come to take leave of him. He received them with his wonted cordiality, and informed them that "This was like to be his last interview with them, at least before his return; that he had ever loved and been kind to them, and ever should continue so to be, not through interest or politic design, but out of real affection; and he desired them, in his absence, to cultivate friendship with those he should leave behind in authority." He informed them that the assembly was then enacting a law, according to their desire, to prevent their being abused by the selling of rum; with which one of the sachems, in the name of the rest, expressed great satisfaction, and desired that the law might be effectually executed.

In the assembly there was considerable altercation between the members from the province and those from the territories, and the governor being about to go to Pennsbury for a few days, sent them the following characteristic letter:

"Friends:—Your union is what I desire, but your peace and accommodation of one another is what I must expect of you. The reputation of it is something, the reality much more; and I desire you to remember and observe what I say—yield in circumstantials to preserve essentials, and being safe in one another, you will always be so in esteem with me. Make me not sad, now I am going to leave you, since 'tis for you as well as for

"Your friend, proprietor, and governor,
"William Penn."

On the governor's return from Pennsbury he signed various laws passed by the assembly, as well as the charter of privileges, which had been read in that body, "and every part thereof approved, agreed to, and thankfully received." This constitution was the last granted to the province and territories, and in some respects was even more liberal than those which preceded it. The principal change was in allowing the assembly to originate bills, and to sit on its own adjournments. It made no provision for the election of a council, which was appointed by the governor, and prohibited from taking cognizance of any complaint relating to property, unless appeals should be provided by law. In regard to civil and religious liberty, the new constitution was as comprehensive as the old one. By a supplementary article, the province and territories were allowed to dissolve their union at any time within three years by giving due notice.

The proprietary, by letters patent, appointed a council of state, consisting of ten members, chiefly Friends, who were to advise and assist him, or his deputy, in the affairs of government, and in case of the deputy's absence or death to exercise the executive functions. In order to give entire satisfaction to the assembly, Penn offered to commission a deputy, whom they should nominate. This offer they took into consideration, but concluded to decline.

At this time, "Friends' Public School," in Philadelphia, which had been incorporated in 1697, received from the governor an amended charter, confirming its privileges. In this excellent institution the poor were taught gratuitously, others paid a part of the expense incurred in their children's education, and it was open on the same terms to all religious persuasions.

Near the time of Penn's departure, a large assemblage of Indian guests met him at Pennsbury, to take leave of him. A council was held in the governor's mansion, where they renewed their former covenants with many expressions of good-will, and promises of continued fidelity. The Indians said "They never first broke covenant with any people, for, as one of them said, and smote his hand upon his head three times, that they did not make them in their heads, but smiting his hand three times on his breast, said they made them there, in their hearts." Presents were made to them by the governor, who spoke to them with much kindness; after which they withdrew to an open space near the house, where they kindled a fire, and around it performed their cantico, or dance, accompanied with songs and shouts of triumph.

The ship being ready to sail, Penn convened the inhabitants of Philadelphia, to take leave of them, on the 29th of October, 1701, when he presented to them a charter or act of incorporation for the city. On the 30th he appointed Andrew Hamilton, formerly governor of East and West Jersey, to be his lieutenant-governor, and James Logan he made provincial secretary and clerk of the council.

Soon after Penn arrived in England he wrote to Logan, saying, "We had a swift passage, 26 days from the Capes to soundings; 30 to Portsmouth. ... Nothing yet done in my affairs, but my coming I do more and more see necessary on divers accounts, though a troublesome and costly journey."

CHAPTER VII.

PENN'S PECUNIARY EMBARRASSMENTS.

1702-1709.

IN the spring of 1702, William III. died, after having made preparations for another war with France, which was declared and prosecuted under his successor. He was considered an able statesman and general, but ambitious of military glory, and so infatuated with the idea of preserving the balance of power in Europe, that he kept England embroiled in expensive continental wars, to the great increase of her debt, the loss of many valuable lives, and the detriment of public morals. He was a sincere friend of religious toleration, and one of his last acts was to sign a bill in favor of the Friends, allowing their solemn affirmation to be accepted instead of an oath.

He was succeeded by Queen Anne, the daughter of James II., and wife of Prince George of Denmark. This princess having, on her accession, publicly declared her intention to maintain the act of toleration in favor of religious dissenters, the yearly meeting of Friends in London adopted an address expressive of their acknowledgments, which was presented to her by William Penn, accompanied by a deputation of Friends.

Soon after Penn's return to England, the bill for converting the proprietary into royal governments, which was before the House of Lords, was withdrawn or defeated; but those who urged the measure did not entirely abandon it; they intended to introduce it into the House of Commons, and all the vigilance and influence of the proprietaries were required to avert the blow or mitigate its force, by obtaining such privileges and immunities as would secure them and the people from the abuse of power.

In a letter to Logan, Penn writes: "The lords of trade have promised me to receive no complaints, without the party sending them give them to the party they are sent against, upon the spot, for their answers, in the nature of bill and answer in chancery, that nobody may be murdered in the dark. A great reformation relief, and for which American governments owe me their good-will."

Although the queen was very favorably disposed towards Penn, there was in Parliament a strong party devoted to the established church and opposed to the liberal government established in Pennsylvania. They alleged that, "in time of war, a province under Quaker rule would invite invasion and conquest, and would furnish a retreat for privateers; that the solemnity of an oath should be required in civil and criminal jurisprudence uniformly throughout all her majesty's dominions. These views were urged and so far prevailed as to induce the parliament to pass an act requiring that the appointment of deputy governors should have the royal assent. Factious opposition was made to the confirmation of Governor Hamilton, it being alleged that he had been engaged in illicit trade. The validity of his acts until confirmed was also questioned. Thus was a most harassing system of opposition to the proprietor's government kept up, every fault being exaggerated, and many mere reports and rumors, void of any foundation in truth, magnified before the eyes of the queen. The appointment of Hamilton finally received the royal confirmation; but so persistent was the opposition to the interests of the proprietor, that he was obliged either to keep an agent or remain himself near the court, to answer the hurtful charges constantly brought against his province and his rule." *

In Pennsylvania there was also a "church

---

* " Lives of the Governors of Pennsylvania," Armor, p. 116.

party," not satisfied with the equality secured to them by the laws of the province, who were disaffected to the proprietary government, and making use of every means in their power to bring it into discredit with the British ministry.

The tolerant and liberal policy of Penn had attracted towards his colony adventurers of every class. All enjoyed equal political privileges; but in the first settlement, the Friends, being much the most numerous, were generally chosen to the legislature and other public stations. In a few years the influx of emigrants, not of their persuasion, was so great that the Friends began to lose their preponderance, and the frequent demands of the British government for aid to military purposes rendered them less willing to serve in public stations. In 1702, the population of the colony was nearly equally divided between Friends and others.

The administration of Governor Hamilton was of short duration, and embittered by dissensions between the representatives of the province and those of the territories, now composing the State of Delaware. The people of the provinces declined to elect representatives to the assembly, at the time fixed by law, and writs being subsequently issued by the governor for an election, they chose delegates, who, when they arrived at the seat of government, refused to unite with the members from the province, claiming their privilege under the charter of dissolving the union. The governor having used every means in his power to reconcile their differences, was at last compelled to dismiss the assembly without the transaction of any business.

Governor Hamilton died the 20th of Second month, 1703; and the executive power devolved on the council, of which Edward Shippen was President. He made an attempt to preserve the union, but the members from the province, who before had been well affected toward it,. then refused to unite with those from the territories, whose refractory conduct, for many years, had exhausted their forbearance. This separation proved final; the province and the territories, thereafter, acted separately in a legislative capacity.

The council soon found themselves involved in difficulty through the machinations of Colonel Robert Quarry, a member of the Church of England, and Judge of the Admiralty, a court established by the British government in her American colonies, for the adjudication of maritime cases. The official station of Colonel Quarry, and that of John Moore, advocate in the same court, rendered them independent of the proprietary and of the colonial legislature, whose views and interests it was their study to thwart in every possible way, but especially by exaggerated reports, transmitted to the Board of Trade, in London.

Colonel Quarry obtained from the queen an order that all the executive and judicial officers of the province should take "the oath directed by the law of England, or the affirmation allowed by the said law to Quakers;". "as also, all persons who, in England, are obliged and willing to take an oath in any public or judicial proceeding, be admitted so to do, by the proper officers and judges in Pennsylvania." Many of the judges and magistrates being Friends, were as scrupulous about administering an oath as taking it themselves. The laws of Pennsylvania did not require it, and a simple affirmation had been sufficient in all judicial proceedings. Now they were required to administer oaths to all who were willing to take them, and rather than comply they would resign their offices, which the church party, under the direction of Quarry and Moore, would gladly occupy.

When information of these proceedings reached the proprietary, he wrote to the council not to regard the demands of Quarry and his party. "For why," he asks, "should you obey any order obtained by the lords of trade, or otherwise, which is not according to patent, nor law here, nor the laws of your own county, which are to govern you till repealed. I desire you to pluck up that English and Christian courage, not to suffer yourselves to be thus treated and put upon. Let those factious fellows do their worst."

He afterwards succeeded in convincing the board of trade that Quarry's proceedings were unjustifiable and turbulent, which caused them to send him a reprimand that silenced him.

The great expenditures incurred by Penn in settling his colony, in defending it against the claims of Lord Baltimore, and in protecting his proprietary rights against the motion in Parliament, together with his family expenses and those of his son, had exhausted his income and loaded him with debt.

His pecuniary wants, together with the embarrassment he experienced from the enemies of proprietary governments in England, and the disaffected among the colonists, induced him to think of selling his government to the crown, but retaining his landed estate in the colony, where he still hoped to spend the evening of his days. In a letter to Logan, in the Fourth month, 1703, he says, "I am actually in treaty with the ministers for my government;" and again, in the Tenth month, he writes, "Fear not my bargain with the crown, for it shall never be made without a security to the inhabitants according to the constitution and laws of the country, though my supplies to defend them come so costly and slowly to my support."

In the early part of the year 1704, John Evans, who had been appointed by Penn, with the queen's approbation, as deputy-governor of Pennsylvania, arrived in Philadelphia. He was recommended, in a letter from Penn to Logan, as "a young man, not above six-and-twenty, but sober and sensible; 'the son of an old friend who loved me not a little.'" He was accompanied by William Penn, Jr., the second and only surviving son of William Penn by his first marriage. Evans was not a Friend, nor even a man of exemplary morals, and Penn must have been much deceived in regard to his character. It is supposed that he was selected through the influence of the party at court, who believed that an efficient government could not be administered upon peace principles, and who would have opposed the confirmation of any deputy holding the views of the Society of Friends.

Soon after the arrival of Governor Evans, he increased the number of members in the provincial council by calling to the board Judge Mompesson, William Trent, Richard Hill, James Logan, and William Penn, Jr. The latter, in honor of his father, was seated next to the governor, but he seldom attended, being more intent upon pleasure than business. Penn, in sending his son to Pennsylvania, placed great reliance on the prudence and good example of James Logan, to whose care he recommended him. The secretary, though a young man himself, fulfilled his trust with wisdom and fidelity, but unhappily this degenerate scion of a noble stock was not to be reclaimed from habits of dissipation into which he had fallen before he left England. He remained but a few months in the colony, and after his return to his home caused his father great solicitude.

Notwithstanding the steps that had been taken to provide separate legislatures for the province and the territories, Governor Evans summoned the representatives of both to meet in Philadelphia, and when they were assembled he made strenuous efforts to unite them in one body, but without success. The assembly of the province, by its unwillingness to enter into the proposed union, incurred the governor's displeasure, which, with the disputes that soon after arose concerning their privileges, occasioned a hostile feeling that obstructed the business of legislation.

Governor Evans having no respect for the peace principles of the proprietary and the Friends, issued a public proclamation for raising a militia, commanding all persons in the colony "whose persuasion would, on any account, permit them to take up arms in their own defence, that forthwith they should provide themselves with a good firelock and ammunition." The reason assigned in the proclamation for this requisition was, that the queen and her allies were "engaged in a vigorous war against France and Spain for maintaining and preserving the liberty and *balance* of Europe."

It was one of the calamitous consequences of subjection to the mother country, that the colonies were involved in her quarrels with other European powers, and especially with France and Spain, whose American possessions, being contiguous to those of Great Britain, brought them into hostile collision. The barbarous policy of the French in subsidizing the Indians and inciting them to murder the frontier settlers, spread alarm and distress, and sometimes resulted in much bloodshed. The Indians of western New York, called the Five Nations, were generally friendly to the English; their authority extended to the Susquehanna; they were on excellent terms with William Penn, and they used their influence with other tribes for the preservation of peace.

The administration of Governor Evans was disturbed throughout nearly its whole course by the conflict of opposing interests and passions. As

PEACE PRINCIPLES EXEMPLIFIED. 145

in all free governments there are usually two or more parties contending for power and watching each other with jealous feelings, so in Pennsylvania there was a party opposed to the proprietary interests, led by David Lloyd, sometime speaker of the assembly, and a party, of which James Logan was the leader, who advocated the rights of William Penn and supported his policy. The first assembly that met after the arrival of Governor Evans had arrested the progress of legislation by its extravagant pretensions, and when the people, dissatisfied with their representatives, elected others qualified and disposed to promote the public good, the harmonious action that ensued was of short duration, for the lieutenant-governor, elated with the triumph of his party, proceeded to acts of dissimulation and oppression that resulted in his own disgrace. He had a strong inclination for military display, and the depredations of privateers and pirates on the commerce of the province, together with the incursions of the Indians in some of the neighboring colonies, furnished him with cogent arguments for enforcing the directions of the British government to put the colony in a posture of defence.

In the lower counties, called the territories, his views met with the concurrence of the people, few of whom were Friends; but in the province, where that peace-loving people were numerous, he found all his efforts to sustain a militia were ineffectual, and only rendered him more unpopular.

Not being able to appreciate the motives of the Friends, and perhaps doubting their sincerity, he determined to put their principles to a severe test, and for that purpose devised a scheme as puerile as it was mischievous.

By an arrangement with an accomplice at New Castle, he managed to have a messenger sent from thence to Philadelphia in great haste and apparent consternation, to notify the authorities and people that a French fleet was coming up the Delaware, and that the town of Lewes was burnt. The militia were called out, and Governor Evans rode about town with his sword drawn, forcing all that could be induced to take arms, and causing powder to be dealt out among the people.

It was the time of the annual fair, and the sudden surprise caused a great commotion. Some of the people threw their plate and other valuable effects into wells, others carried away what they could, and the vessels and boats in the harbor were taken up the river. The Friends, instead of being driven to arms in this supposed emergency, evinced by their calmness and self-possession the firmness of their principles. It being the day of their mid-week meeting for worship, they assembled at the meeting-house as usual, and, regardless of the general tumult, engaged in their accustomed devotion.

Soon after the alarm, the assembly was convened, when Governor Evans stated to them his views on the propriety of establishing a militia and erecting fortifications; but they replied that they had levied a considerable tax last year for the support of government; that their crops having failed and their trade decayed, they were unable to do more; and they earnestly desired of the governor, that those who brought up the false reports by which the alarm was caused might be brought "to condign punishment."

The indignation of the inhabitants at the governor's conduct was greatly increased by an unwarrantable attempt he made to levy an impost on their commerce. Having induced the assembly of the territories to pass a law for the erection of a fort at New Castle, the masters of all vessels navigating the Delaware were required to report themselves, and inward-bound vessels were subjected to a duty of half-a-pound of powder for every ton of their capacity.

This illegal exaction was highly resented by the merchants, being in contravention of the royal charter which secured to them the free navigation of the river. Richard Hill, Samuel Preston, and William Fishborn, owners of a new sloop, called the "Philadelphia," then leaving on her first voyage to Barbadoes, determined to withstand the exaction, and acquainting the governor with their purpose, went on board.

The governor hastened to New Castle and ordered watch to be kept for the vessel. As she approached, she anchored above the fort, where Preston and Fishborn went ashore and informed John French, the commandant of the fort, that she was regularly cleared, and they demanded their right to pass without interruption. This being refused, Richard Hill, who had been bred to the sea, took the helm and steered past the fort, with no other injury than a shot through the main-sail. French pursued in an armed boat, and coming alongside, they cast him a rope by means of which he boarded the vessel, when those on board cut the rope, which caused the boat to fall astern, and making him a prisoner without a blow, they proceeded on their way. The governor, greatly exasperated, pursued them in another boat to Salem, where Richard Hill went ashore with his prisoner; and Lord Cornbury, governor of New Jersey, being there, who claimed to be vice-admiral of the river Delaware, they brought the matter before him. He sharply reproved French for his conduct, and to Governor Evans he expressed his disapprobation.

Hill and his associates were members of the Society of Friends; they stood high in the community, and their conduct was generally approved.

At the next meeting of the legislature, they presented a petition on the subject, which occasioned a remonstrance from that body to the governor on his illegal proceedings.

The misconduct of Evans being communicated to the proprietary by letters from Logan and by a remonstrance from the assembly, his removal was deemed necessary, and Charles Gookin was appointed deputy-governor, in the year 1709.

While Penn was struggling with the difficulties attendant on his station as proprietary, and burdened with sorrow from the dereliction of his son, he was subjected to the most galling pecuniary embarrassments by the treachery of his steward. Philip Ford was a man of respectable standing, a member of the Society of Friends, and much esteemed by Penn, who employed him in the management of his estates, placing implicit confidence in his integrity, and accepting his accounts without scrutiny. It was this easy, confiding temper, so amiable in itself, that led the proprietary into many of the difficulties he encountered.

On the large sums of money that passed through his hands for many years he charged exorbitant commissions, and on his advances he calculated compound interest every six months at eight per cent., which was one-third more than the law allowed, by which means, although he had received seventeen thousand pounds and expended sixteen thousand only, he brought the proprietary in debt to the amount of ten thousand five hundred pounds. Penn, from time to time, accepted his accounts without sufficient examination, and finally, to secure the debt, gave him a lien upon his province in the form of a deed of conveyance.

After the death of Philip Ford, his widow and son Philip brought suit, and Penn, not being able to satisfy their demands, became a prisoner for debt. He offered, for "peace sake," to pay such a sum as disinterested men might award, but the prosecutors were inexorable, and he continued about nine months within the prison bounds. During his imprisonment his friends exerted themselves for his relief, and the sum of seven thousand six hundred pounds being raised, it was accepted in liquidation of the claim, and he was again set at liberty.

Throughout the whole of this vexatious and humiliating business he evinced the fortitude of a true Christian, whose affections were fixed, not on earthly but on heavenly things; and the beautiful remark of his friend, Isaac Norris, seemed applicable to him: "God darkens this world to us, that our eyes may behold the greater brightness of his kingdom."

CHAPTER VIII.

THE LAST DAYS OF PENN.

1700-1718.

WHEN Governor Gookin arrived in Philadelphia the assembly then in session presented him an address signed by David Lloyd, their speaker, in which, unhappily, they not only alluded to the conduct of his immediate predecessor, but requested that he might be prosecuted and punished for malversation in office, and they intimated that he had been influenced by "*evil counsel*," to which they attributed his obnoxious measures. The governor prudently declined to comply with their request, and an angry contest arose between the council, charged with being accessory to the misdeeds of Evans, and the assembly, which was urgent for the prosecution.

In obedience to an order from the queen, the governor made a requisition upon the assembly for assistance toward a military expedition against Canada. The quota required from Pennsylvania was one hundred and fifty men and a contribution in money. The governor stated to the house, that being aware of the scruples of many of the inhabitants against bearing arms, he would excuse them from furnishing troops if they would raise a subsidy of four thousand pounds. After much debate, the assembly replied that they could not, for conscience sake, comply with the requisition, but in gratitude to the queen for her many favors, they had resolved to raise and present her with five hundred pounds as a testimony of their loyalty. This was by no means satisfactory to the governor, who insisted upon a larger sum, and the assembly subsequently offered to add three hundred pounds for a present to the Indians and other public charges, and two hundred pounds for the governor's salary, expecting in return his concurrence in redressing their grievances. The governor resented this condition as a want of confidence and courtesy, and the remainder of the session was spent in fruitless debates and messages.

On the last day of the session, the assembly adopted another remonstrance containing heavy charges against Logan, intended, as he believed, for political effect, as he was not then allowed to answer it, and they had it publicly read in the several counties on the day of election.

In the next assembly, which met in October,

1709, the same party was predominant, and David Lloyd was again chosen speaker.

Logan, who had hitherto stood on the defensive, now became the assailant, and preferred, through the governor, charges against Lloyd for high misdemeanors. He at the same time demanded a trial on the accusations made against himself, and stated that he was about to embark for England. The assembly, instead of attempting to prove their charges, passed a resolution for his arrest and imprisonment, but the governor issued a supersedeas to prevent the execution of the speaker's writ, and Logan embarked for England. It appears that after a full hearing there, he was triumphantly acquitted, "both by Friends and the civil authorities."

The confidence of William Penn in his secretary never wavered; and even in the province a reaction took place soon after his departure. The friends of the proprietary rallied; the eyes of the people were opened to the deceptions that had been practised upon them, and Lloyd's party was completely prostrated.

In the election of 1710, not a single member of the last assembly was returned; all were friends of the proprietary; they chose Richard Hill for their speaker, and their proceedings were characterized by order, decorum and despatch.

Soon after the election, an expostulatory letter was received from Penn, written before he had heard of the reaction in favor of his government. It is composed in a strain of serious admonition, and its effect was most salutary; being a beautiful exposition of his affectionate regard and paternal care for the people of his province.

By the election of the new assembly, harmony was restored to the government, and all its branches were distinguished by sedulous and successful application to business. The expenses of the State were cheerfully supplied, and the judiciary was established on a satisfactory basis. The voice of complaint was hushed, while the manifold blessings enjoyed by the inhabitants were frankly acknowledged.

In 1711, another requisition was made by the British government for aid in prosecuting the war against Canada, which being communicated by the governor to the assembly, they, after some delay, passed a law for "raising two thousand pounds to the queen's use."

There is extant a letter of Isaac Norris in reference to this law, in which he says: "We did not see it inconsistent with our principles to give the queen money, notwithstanding any use she might put it to, *that* not being our part, but hers."

In the year 1712, the ascendency of the Friends

in the assembly is indicated by the passage of "an act to prevent the importation of negroes and Indians into the province." But this wise and humane law was annulled by the crown, in pursuance of that nefarious policy of the British government, which sought to enrich her merchants by keeping open, in her colonies, a market for men.

It is pleasing to reflect, that during the last three years of William Penn's participation in colonial affairs, harmony prevailed in the government of his province, and that an act so consonant with his feelings and principles was then passed; for though at that time unsuccessful, it entitles Pennsylvania to the honorable distinction of having led the way to a more humane system of legislation on the subject of slavery.

For some years Penn had been negotiating with the British cabinet for the sale of his government. He was impelled to this step by two principal motives; the first arose from pecuniary embarrassments—the province being still under a mortgage to those friends who released him from his debt to the Fords; the second was the difficulty he found in his administration, being on the one hand often thwarted by a faction in the colony, and on the other restrained, by his allegiance to the crown, from the full development of his peaceable policy. Perhaps a third motive may have been the unfitness of his eldest son to succeed him as proprietary and governor.

There were, however, other considerations which inclined him to keep his government: the original purpose of the enterprise was to found a "free colony for all mankind," and to administer its government on Christian principles. This favorite idea had been more nearly realized than in any other instance on record; and he still indulged the hope that if a peace were concluded in Europe, and he settled with his family at Pennsbury, he might yet see all his plans accomplished, and spend the evening of his days in tranquillity.

Another strong motive for retaining the government was to secure for the Friends in Pennsylvania that religious liberty which had been one of their main inducements to emigrate. This object, together with political privileges for the people, he kept constantly in view during his negotiations with the cabinet, by which means the completion of the contract was delayed for some years.

The advice of Logan and some of his best friends was in favor of the sale, though they regretted the necessity that seemed to require it. In the summer of 1712, the terms of the surrender were agreed upon, the price being fixed at twelve thousand pounds, payable in four years, but the conveyance was not then executed. In the autumn of the same year he was attacked by paralysis, while writing to James Logan. It came upon him so suddenly that his hand was arrested in the beginning of a sentence, which he never completed.

He was then at Bristol, and recovered sufficiently to go to London, and thence to his residence at Ruscombe.

During six years he lingered an invalid, gradually sinking to the grave. His memory was impaired, his noble intellect was clouded, but the sweetness of his temper remained, and he was favored to retain the highest and best of his endowments—a sense of spiritual enjoyment, and a heart overflowing with love to God and man.

He had received a thousand pounds in advance on the sale of his government, but the deed not being executed, the crown lawyers gave it as their opinion that he was not capable of completing the surrender. In this emergency the whole burden of his public and private affairs devolved on his wife.

Hannah Penn was a woman of extraordinary energy and fortitude; her arduous duties were faithfully and successfully performed; the return of peace, in 1713, brought prosperity to the colony; the increasing value of property there enabled her, after some years, to discharge the mortgage; and during her husband's declining health, the voice of complaint was seldom heard from the assembly or people of Pennsylvania.

On the 30th day of the Fifth month (July, O. S.), 1718, William Penn passed from the trials of time to the rewards of eternity; being in the 74th year of his age. He was buried at Jordans, in Buckinghamshire, where his first wife and several of his family had been before interred.

Hannah Penn received from "the General Meeting" of Friends, in Philadelphia, an affectionate letter of condolence; and the Indians in Pennsylvania, hearing of the death of their great and good friend Onas, in order to testify their regard for his memory, and their sympathy with his widow, sent her an address of condolence, accompanied by a present. It consisted of "materials for a garment of skins, suitable for travelling through a thorny wilderness," intending to express by this symbol the difficulties that lay in her path, and their desire that she might pass through them in safety.

In all the transactions of his eventful life, the character of William Penn shines out in clearness and purity. The lapse of more than one hundred and fifty years has not dimmed its lustre, and even his modern traducer admits that "his name has become, throughout all civilized countries, a synonym for probity and philanthropy."*

---

* For a refutation of Macaulay's charges against William Penn, see W. E. Forster's "Preface to Clarkson's Life of

One of the most remarkable traits in his character was his magnanimity. With singular disregard for selfish or personal considerations, he devoted his life to the good of mankind. When we consider the sacrifices he made for the benefit of others, we cannot but lament that the evening of his days was clouded by pecuniary embarrassments. Had he been careful to husband the revenues of his Irish estates, had he not generously declined the imposts offered him by the first colonial assembly, had he been less charitable to the poor, and less bountiful to the Indians, he might have lived in affluence, and been saved the humiliation of imprisonment for debt. But would his character have been more dear to our hearts? Should we not have missed some of the most instructive portions of his history? As in prosperity he was not vainly elated, so, in adversity, he was not unduly depressed, but evinced in all his vicissitudes a happy equanimity. In the counsels of infinite wisdom, his afflictions were, doubtless, made instrumental to some high purpose; perhaps to purify the immortal spirit for its blest abode, or to mani-

---

Penn;" W. Hepworth Dixon's "Historical Biography of Penn;" S. M. Janney's "Life of Penn," chap. xxii., and appendix to edition 4th, and subsequent editions: "An Inquiry into the evidence relating to the charges brought by Lord Macaulay against William Penn," by John Paget, Esq., Barrister-at-law, London, 1858.

fest to the world the power of religion to sustain the soul under all the trials of life.

It is remarked by Bancroft, that "Penn never gave counsel at variance with popular rights." . . . "England to-day confesses his sagacity, and is doing honor to his genius." "After more than a century, the laws which he reproved began gradually to be repealed; and the principle which he developed, sure of immortality, is slowly, but firmly, asserting its power over the legislation of Great Britain." . . . . "Every charge of hypocrisy, of selfishness, of vanity, of dissimulation, of credulous confidence; every form of reproach, from virulent abuse to cold apology, every ill name, from tory and Jesuit, to blasphemer and infidel, has been used against Penn; but the candor of his character always triumphed over calumny.

"His name was safely cherished as a household word in the cottages of Wales and Ireland, and among the peasantry of Germany; and not a tenant of a wigwam, from the sea to the Susquehanna, doubted his integrity. His fame is now wide as the world; he is one of the few who have gained abiding glory." *

---

* "History of United States," II., 381–400.

CHAPTER IX.

THE PEACE-POLICY A SUCCESS.

IT was the purpose of William Penn and his associates to found and govern a commonwealth, without arms or military defences, in accordance with the peace principles enunciated by our Saviour in his sermon on the mount.

We can readily conceive that such an experiment, if attempted on an island, previously uninhabited, not subject to foreign control, and colonized by men imbued with the principles of peace, would probably succeed in securing a degree of harmony and happiness not elsewhere to be found on earth. But in Pennsylvania the case was widely different. Owing allegiance to the British government, whose policy was warlike and aggressive, vehemently urged by the officers of the crown to join the other colonies in their hostilities against the French and Indians; having a British court of admiralty established in her midst; endeavoring to exact the use of oaths; and worst of all, having in her metropolis a band of adventurers, attracted thither by her prosperity, abusing the liberty they enjoyed and fomenting discord, in order to weaken the proprietary government—that with all these impediments, William Penn should have succeeded in maintaining his authority without a compromise of his principles, may be accounted truly wonderful.

A government can be conducted on the principles of peace, by those only who have an abiding faith in Divine protection, and forbear to provide themselves with military defences. This position is sustained by reference to the history of the other American colonies.

"In Maryland, as well as in New England," says Graham, in his "Colonial History," "doubtless the pacific endeavors of the colonists were counteracted, not only by the natural ferocity of the Indians, but by the hostilities of other Europeans, by which that ferocity was, from time to time, enkindled and developed. Yet the Quakers of Pennsylvania, who were exposed to the same disadvantage, escaped its evil consequences, and were never attacked by the Indians.

"Relying implicitly and exclusively on the protection of Heaven, they renounced every act or indication of self-defence that could awaken the contentiousness of human nature, or excite apprehensive jealousy by ostentation of the power to injure. But the Puritan and Catholic colonists of New England and Maryland, while they professed and exercised good-will to the Indians, adopted the hostile precaution of demonstrating their readiness and ability to repel violence. They displayed arms and erected forts, and thus provoked the suspicion they expressed, and invited the injury they anticipated."

It would not be difficult to point out a dangerous fallacy in the maxim so generally believed—that in time of peace nations should prepare for war. For as in the intercourse of individuals with each other, it is found that those who habitually carry arms are more liable than others to be involved in deadly affrays, so in the intercourse of nations, the hostile attitude assumed by their vast armaments, and the numerous officers employed, who are dependent for promotion and renown on actual hostilities, are rather incentives to war than sureties for peace.

The enterprise of Penn and his associates in the colony of Pennsylvania, by demonstrating the feasibility of peaceable principles, has served to confirm the faith of the wavering, and to encourage the true-hearted disciples of Christ. As an example of Christian principles applied to the government of a commonwealth, it stands without a parallel in the history of the world; and will, doubtless, continue to be more admired and imitated as time advances, until that happy period shall arrive when "nation shall not lift up sword against nation, neither shall they learn war any more."

The political contests which, at times, disturbed the harmony of the colony, and caused much solicitude to the Founder, though considered at the time portentous evils, were such as frequently are found in all free governments. The people were sometimes misled by designing demagogues, but when their minds were disabused, and they were aroused to action, a strong majority was found on the side of order. "To freedom and justice a fair field was given, and they were safe."

There was, in the charter of Pennsylvania, a defect which Penn could neither avoid nor remedy. He was a feudal sovereign, acting as the executive of a democracy, and these two elements were found incompatible. While residing in the colony, his sweetness of temper, and weight of character, enabled him to govern without encountering factious opposition, but, in his absence, no deputy could be found fully competent to supply his place. But although the passions and frailties incident to human nature gave rise, at times, to contention, and obstructed the course of legislation, there was no resort to arms, and all the dreadful calamities of war were averted.

There is no evidence on the records that the death-penalty for crime was inflicted—human life was held sacred—and the reformation of offenders was considered an important end in the administration of punitive justice.

There were many settlements of Indians in Bucks and Chester counties, which remained long after the foundation of the colony. "Tradition relates that they were kind neighbors, supplying the white people with meat and sometimes with beans and other vegetables, which they did in perfect charity, bringing presents to their houses and refusing pay. Their children were sociable and fond of play; a harmony arose out of their mutual intercourse and dependence, and native simplicity reigned to its greatest extent." *

The efforts of the Friends to benefit the Indians were not confined to endeavors to conciliate and civilize them, but extended to their instruction in spiritual knowledge, and the practice of a Christian life. These efforts were not without success, for although few of the natives embraced the Christian profession, there is abundant evidence that many among them evinced, by their deportment, some of the noblest traits of the Christian character. There is an account of "a portion of them in the

---

* Manuscript account by Dr. John Watson, in the archives of the Historical Society, Pa.

western part of Pennsylvania, who, from a self-conviction of the injustice and irreligion of war, united themselves into a community, with a resolution to war no more; and asserting as their reason that 'when God made men, he did not intend they should hurt or kill one another.'" This account is given by Anthony Benezet, and he attributes the wonderful change in their deportment to the immediate operation of the " light of Christ in the soul."

The natives, on their part, did not fail to reciprocate the benevolence of the colonists. Though generally prompt to avenge an injury, they never forgot a kindness, and were not surpassed by any other people in the virtues of gratitude, honesty and veracity.

During the whole time the influence of the Friends prevailed in the province, being a period of more than seventy years, the Indians in Pennsylvania seldom committed an injury, and never took the life of a white man.

"Of all the colonies that ever existed," says Ebeling, "none was ever founded on so philanthropic a plan, none was so deeply impressed with the character of its founder, none practised in a greater degree the principles of toleration, liberty and peace, and none rose and flourished more rapidly than Pennsylvania. She was the youngest of the British colonies established before the eighteenth century, but it was not long before she surpassed most of her elder sisters in population, agriculture, and general prosperity." *

This sentiment is corroborated by the eloquent language of Charles Sumner: "To William Penn," he says, "belongs the distinction, destined to brighten as men advance in virtue, of first in human history establishing the *Law of Love* as a rule of conduct in intercourse of nations. He declined the superfluous protection of arms against foreign force, and 'aimed to reduce the savage nations by just and gentle manners to the love of civil society and the Christian religion.' His serene countenance, as he stands with his followers, all unarmed, beneath the spreading elm, forming the great treaty of friendship with the untutored Indians—who fill with savage display the surrounding forest as far as the eye can reach—not to wrest their lands by violence, but to obtain them by peaceful purchase, is to my mind the proudest picture in the history of our country. 'The great God,' said the illustrious Quaker, 'has written his law in our hearts by which we are taught and commanded to love, and to help, and to do good to one another. It is not our

---

* " History of Pennsylvania," by Professor Ebeling, of Hamburg. "Hazard's Reg.," I., 340.

custom to use hostile weapons against our fellow-creatures, for which reason we have come unarmed; our object is not to do injury, but to do good. We have, then, met in the broad pathway of good faith and good-will, so that no advantage can be taken on either side, but all is to be openness, brotherhood and love, while all are to be treated as of the same flesh and blood.' These are words of true greatness. The flowers of prosperity smile in the blessed footprints of William Penn. His people were unmolested and happy, while—sad contrast—those of other colonies, acting upon the policy of the world, building forts, and showing themselves in arms, not after receiving provocation, but merely in anticipation, or from fear of danger, were harassed by perpetual alarm, and pierced by the sharp arrows of savage war. This pattern of a Christian commonwealth never fails to arrest the admiration of all who contemplate its beauties."

THE END.

LATE PUBLICATIONS

BY

FRIENDS' BOOK ASSOCIATION,

706 ARCH STREET,

PHILADELPHIA.

A NEW EDITION OF THE

LIFE OF WM. PENN.

By SAML. M. JANNEY.

With a complete Index. Fine Cloth. Price, $1.25

LIFE OF GEO. FOX.

By SAML. M. JANNEY.

Price, Cloth, $1.00

THE HOME CIRCLE.

By ANN S. PASCHALL.

Suitable for First Day Schools and Libraries. Fine Cloth, $1.00.

"SELECTED POEMS."

A choice selection of Poems for the Young, and for First Day Schools and Libraries. Price, Cloth, 50c.

www.ingramcontent.com/pod-product-compliance
Lightning Source LLC
Chambersburg PA
CBHW020306170426
43202CB00008B/520